2-50

A SECOND LOOK
at
HARMONY

by TIBOR SERLY

SAMUEL FRENCH
Incorporated

FORRELL, THOMAS & POLACK
Associates, Incorporated

NEW YORK, N.Y.

SAMUEL FRENCH, INC.
25 West 45th Street, New York, N.Y.

FORRELL, THOMAS & POLACK ASSOCIATES, INC.
157 West 57th Street, New York, N.Y.

To Zoltan Kodaly
To whom I owe much of what I
have learned about music.

Credits

We are grateful to the music publishers listed below for their kind permission to include in this volume excerpts from the following copyrighted material:

Preface

Music is not, of course, an exact science, nor can its techniques ever remain static. And since it is axiomatic that practice precedes theory, it was natural for theorists to keep abreast of new harmonic developments which could not be readily accounted for in the earlier "austere" classical methods. Therefore, adjustments were made from time to time to conform with creative development. This was especially the case during the period of transition from post-romantic music to impressionistic music.

But toward the end of the nineteenth century a daring spurt was manifest in the harmonic idiom. Many rules previously established were either completely ignored or deliberately broken by the most talented composers. It was then that harmony should have been reduced to its bare essentials, carefully scrutinized and re-evaluated. Instead, theorists, finding themselves in a quandary to define these strange and new manifestations, tampered with the basic principles of harmony. As a consequence, the teaching of harmony and chord structures underwent a radical change from its original *diatonic* concept to a *chromatic* one. Ignoring almost entirely its diatonic bases, much of the pedagogy of "modern harmony" became a chaotic mixture of chromatic and enharmonic elements.

Today, we stand at the crossroads between the past, the unsolved present and the problematic future. Harmony originally grew out of the modal systems by evolutionary processes. Harmony proved by its performance for over four centuries that it was founded upon natural laws of musical sound. The need is urgent for us to review harmony stripped of all its trappings, so that it may be more closely compared to its practice by the classical and romantic composers when harmony was a *living, contemporaneous technique.*

There is a growing conviction among many musicians that the connection between classical harmony and contemporary dissonance may be closer than has been supposed. In the meantime, until a universally acceptable method is evolved which can explain and account for *all* contemporary harmonic practice (as harmony did for all classical music), it is my contention that one can gain more insight into the present, as well as the future, by "a second look at harmony."

Introduction

Parts I, II and III of this book primarily constitute a treatise on traditional harmony. Part IV ("Harmony Problems Old and New") deals with some of the more speculative aspects of harmony. It also serves as an introduction to the author's theory embodied in his "MODUS LASCIVUS."*

Instead of quoting profuse musical excerpts, which at once intrigue more than instruct the reader, here a different approach has been chosen with the objective of giving as complete a picture as possible of all harmonic matter pertinent to *basic* chords and chord structures, analyzed step by step. The few exercises given are highly concentrated and have been so graded that unless each move is carefully executed, one is certain to be trapped into making faulty progressions. The contents may be best described as a concentrated exposition of harmony with appropriate technical illustrations. This applies especially to *diatonic modulation,* considered by the author to be the core of harmony.

TIBOR SERLY

---

* Now in preparation for publication.

Acknowledgements

I am greatly indebted to Carl Signon for his valuable assistance in many ways. To Ernest Carnicelli and Gerald Serly for attending to various details. Also to Miriam Molin, who meticulously prepared and compiled the index. My special thanks to Mark Bucci for his advice on the musical excerpts, and for editing the publication. Also to Henry Pleasants and Paul Vajda for their helpful suggestions in reading the manuscript. And my sincere thanks to Messrs. Forrell, Thomas & Polack Associates, and Samuel French, Inc., Publishers, for their generous support. I am most grateful, too, to the many professional students of mine, past and present, who encouraged me to carry out this project.

Contents

PART I

DIATONIC PROCESSES

Section One

DIATONIC PROCESSES

Section Two

PART II

CHROMATIC PROCESSES

PART III

ENHARMONIC PROCESSES

"To the *diatonic* falls what is pleasant; to the *chromatic* what is varied; the *enharmonic* upsets the air, carries to excess all our passions—frightens, terrifies, and scatters disorder."

J. P. RAMEAU*

PART ONE

DIATONIC PROCESSES

Section One

I. Preliminaries

HARMONY, and in fact all Western music, may be classified into three distinct categories: DIATONIC, CHROMATIC and ENHARMONIC. In the ensuing chapters each one of these three elements is treated separately.

Part one is concerned exclusively with the understanding and application of diatonic harmony.

Diatonic Harmony

DIATONIC means the use of tones and chords confined to the major and minor scales. Specifically, only the seven tones of the major scale can be classified as purely diatonic. Broadly speaking, however, music that is generally limited to a diatonic background is considered diatonic music. This includes the music of the great classical era of Haydn, Mozart, Beethoven and Schubert.

In the modern sense HARMONY is the science of chords and their normal relationships. Harmony and its disciplines cannot be examined without first defining intervals and the scales from which harmony and chords originate. INTERVAL signifies the difference in pitch between two tones, and is determined by counting the scale degrees from the lowest to the highest.

* Traité de l'harmonie (Translated by W. O. Strunk; *Source Readings in Music History*—W. W. Norton & Co., N.Y. 1950).

Thus, an interval is harmonic when simultaneously sounded, and melodic when one interval follows the other (shown in dark notes).

Furthermore, intervals as employed in traditional harmony may be defined as belonging in two classifications: CONSONANCE and DISSONANCE. Consonant intervals are those which can stand alone and need no resolution. Dissonant intervals, on the other hand, are incomplete—leave one hanging in the air—and require resolution into a consonance.

Consonant intervals are: perfect unisons, octaves, fourths and fifths; and both major and minor thirds and sixths. Dissonant intervals are: major and minor sevenths, major and minor seconds, and all augmented and diminished intervals.

Intervals of the Major Scale

The chart shows the seven tones of the diatonic major scale in whole notes, with the five added chromatic tones in parenthetic shaded notes. For the present we need consider only the major scale.

Ex. 1

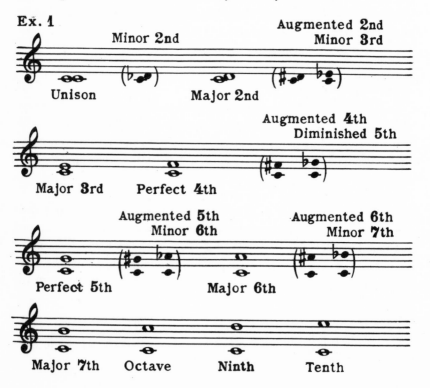

Intervals are called simple up to the octave, and compound when they extend beyond the octave. Thus, a second plus an octave is a ninth; an octave plus a third is a tenth, etc.

From C to C = a unison or prime (both notes are on the same tone)
     C to D = a major second (one whole tone)
     C to E = a major third (two whole tones)
     C to F = a perfect fourth (two tones and a half)
     C to G = a perfect fifth (three tones and a half)
     C to A = a major sixth (four tones and a half)
     C to B = a major seventh (five tones and a half)
     C to C = an octave (six tones)
     C to D 8va = a ninth
     C to E 8va = a tenth

Degrees of the Scale

The seven degrees of the scale are indicated by Roman numerals and each degree has a name.

I   —tonic
II   —supertonic
III —mediant
IV   —subdominant
V   —dominant
VI   —submediant
VII—leading tone

Chords and Triads

A CHORD is a combination of two or more different tones simultaneously sounded.

Most theorists consider three or more different tones simultaneously sounded to be a chord. But aural tests reveal that chords of only two different tones, when doubled in octaves, sound more chordal than a triad consisting of three dissimilar tones.

4

Ex. 2

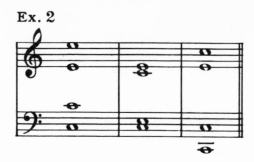

Traditional harmony primarily concerns the study of chords arranged as triads.

A TRIAD is a chord consisting of three tones each separated by a third. The lowest tone is called the *root* or fundamental, the middle tone, the *third,* and the upper tone, the *fifth.*

Ex. 3

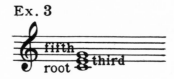

There are four kinds of triads: major, minor, diminished and augmented (abbreviated: maj., min., dim., aug.). They are so named because of the intervallic distance between the tones of the triad.

Ex. 4

Major   Minor   Diminished   Augmented

A major triad consists of the root, maj. third, and perfect fifth.
A minor triad consists of the root, min. third, and perfect fifth.
A diminished triad consists of the root, min. third, and dim. fifth.
An augmented triad consists of the root, maj. third, and aug. fifth.

Note: Major and minor triads are considered *perfect* triads; the diminished and augmented are *imperfect.*

Triads of the Major Scale

Three of the four kinds of triads occur on each degree of the major scale.

Ex. 5

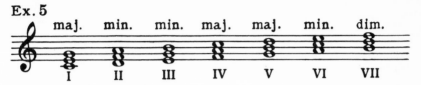

On I the triad is major
On II the triad is minor
On III the triad is minor
On IV the triad is major
On V the triad is major
On VI the triad is minor
On VII the triad is diminished

Thus, the triads on I, IV and V are major, on II, III and VI, minor; and on VII, the diminished. The major scale does not have an augmented triad.

Key Signatures

The sharps or flats appearing at the beginning of each staff denote the key or tonality of a composition. A given signature indicates one of two keys, a major key or its relative minor. These are designated in the accompanying illustration by a whole note for major, and a shaded note for minor.

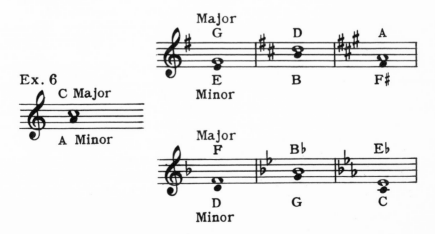

There are twelve major and twelve minor keys proper. The last three sharp keys (both major and their relative minor) are synonymous with the three last flat keys. Therefore, C sharp major is equivalent to D flat, F sharp to G flat, and B is the same as C flat major, etc.

2. Four-Part Writing

HARMONY exercises are traditionally written in four parts on two staves. The perfect prototype for writing in four voices may be best observed in any chorale by J. S. Bach.

The 371 chorales by BACH have been called *The Bible of Harmonization*. Each voice is contrapuntally conceived and the laws regarding harmonic and melodic progressions are, for the most part, strictly applied. It is all the more remarkable that most of the chorales were harmonized before the present rules dealing with chords and their inversions were proven by JEAN PHILIPPE RAMEAU in his famous *Traité de L'harmonie* (written ca. 1723).

Ex. 7

But even four-part barbershop harmony basically adheres to the same principle.

Ex. 8

It should be remembered that harmony evolved principally from vocal music. As instrumental music gradually superseded vocal music, harmony and its strict laws underwent modification. Thus, although harmony is still taught according to the older method of vocal writing —and correctly so—it is mainly applied to instrumental writing since the early part of the nineteenth century.

"The contrast between vocal and instrumental styles may well have been decisive in the fundamental contrast between melodic and harmonic concepts. A survey of the music of ancient Greece and the Orient shows very distinctly that the need for harmony develops with instruments more easily than with voices."*

Harmony primarily concerns the basic operation of chords, the part of music that most closely approaches exact science. This being so, it should be learned for itself, *apart from melodic and harmonic considerations.* (See P. 12.) Treatises that attempt to teach harmony today by means of compositional examples, except to illustrate a BASIC HARMONIC PROGRESSION, may beguile the student, but also easily lead to false conclusions.

Open and Close Position

There are two ways of separating or spacing the four voices in harmony exercises. 1) CLOSE POSITION. Close position, for our purposes, means that three of the voices, soprano, alto and tenor are written in the upper staff. And the remaining voice, the bass, in the lower staff.

Ex. 9

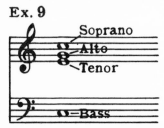

In close position it is recommended that none of the upper voices be separated by more than an octave.

Ex. 10

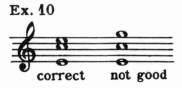

correct   not good

* Curt Sachs: *The Rise of Music in the Ancient World*—W. W. Norton & Co., N.Y.

The distance between the bass and its nearest voice in the upper staff, the tenor, may extend to the limit of two octaves.

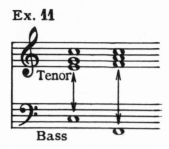

Ex. 11

2) OPEN POSITION. Open position distributes the four voices equally. Soprano and alto in the upper staff, and tenor and bass in the lower staff.

Ex. 12

Range of Voices

In harmony exercises in open position the four parts generally adhere to their equivalent vocal range, as shown in Example 13.

Ex. 13

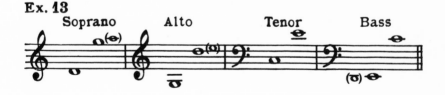

In close position, however, it is almost impossible to exceed the vocal range if the simple rules of voice leading are observed.

Movement of Voices

There are three kinds of directional motion: parallel, contrary and oblique.

PARALLEL MOTION: (a) two or more voices moving in the same direction.

CONTRARY MOTION: (b) two or more voices moving in opposite motion.

OBLIQUE MOTION: (c) one voice or more remaining stationary while others move.

Ex. 14

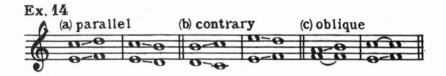

Position of the Upper Voice

Harmony exercises usually commence with the tonic triad, with the root in the soprano, and the bass. However, an exercise may occasionally begin with the third or fifth in the soprano. When the root is highest, it is in *position* of *octave*, abbreviated, pos-8. When the third is highest, it is in *position* of *third*, pos-3. And when the fifth is highest, it is in *position* of *fifth*, pos-5. The position of a chord, unless otherwise specified, refers only to the highest tone of the *first* triad.

Ex. 15

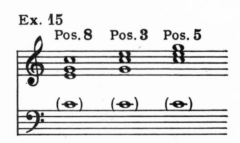

3. Rules of Harmonic Progression

RULES FOR avoiding faulty progressions are few in number, but vital to correct part-writing. The most important of these are listed below.

Parallel Octaves and Fifths

Avoid parallel (or consecutive) octaves and fifths. This means that any two voices moving in the same direction in octaves or fifths, either up or down, are considered faulty.

Ex. 16

Ex. 17

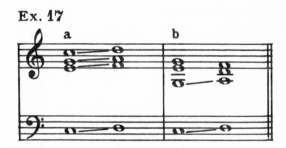

a) contains both parallel fifths and octaves.
b) has consecutive fifths between the tenor and bass.

Some harmony books simply say that consecutive octaves and fifths are disallowed because they make bad music. However, the main reason for avoiding consecutive octaves and fifths in harmonic progressions is to achieve independence of voice movement. A parallel octave is the doubling of the same tone, and hence does not constitute an independent move. Consecutive fifths have much the same effect.

Melodic versus Harmonic Progressions

Theorists often confuse MELODIC moves with HARMONIC progressions.

Ex. 18   A. Dvorak-Valse in D♭

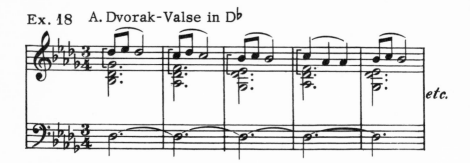

etc.

The above example has been cited to prove that the principle of consecutive fifths—as being a faulty progression—has been long passé. In Example 18, however, the melody itself comprises a separate entity from the harmonic background. An examination of the four-part harmony below the melody reveals a Db pedal in the bass, over which three upper voices move in perfect agreement with rules of traditional harmony. In musical analysis, we should separate the *melodic* from the *harmonic* elements.

Hidden Octaves and Fifths

When two tones progressing in similar motion arrive simultaneously at an octave or a perfect fifth, HIDDEN or COVERED octaves (or fifths) are formed.

Ex. 19

Hidden octaves   Hidden fifths

In strict counterpoint there are specific restrictions regarding these intervals. In four-part harmony there is quite a divergence of opinion among theorists as to which are objectionable and which are not. So far as we are concerned, if the few strict harmony rules listed are observed, the occurrence of objectionable progressions of this kind is negligible.

Augmented Skips

An augmented skip in any individual voice, either upward or down, is considered faulty.

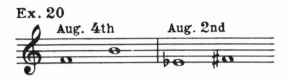

All augmented intervals (a) become diminished when they are inverted, (b).

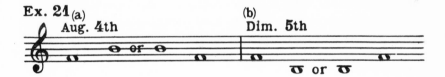

Skips of diminished intervals are permitted, and the tones in an augmented interval are acceptable only when inverted to diminished.

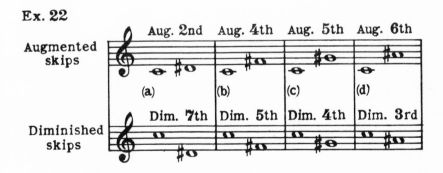

a) aug. seconds become dim. sevenths
b) aug. fourths become dim. fifths
c) aug. fifths become dim. fourths
d) aug. sixths become dim. thirds.

Diminished skips upward generally resolve to the tone immediately below it;

Ex. 22 a

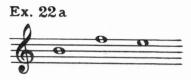

diminished skips downward resolve a semitone up.

Ex. 22 b

Other skips to be avoided are major and minor sixths, and major and minor sevenths (see exception in exchange of the same chord, P. 21).

Common Tones

When a tone, sometimes two, is retained by the same voice in the next chord, it is called a common or connecting tone.

Ex. 23

at a) the soprano voice is retained in the second chord.

at b) the G in the alto voice is held over.

at c) Here two common tones, both C in the soprano and A in the alto are retained.

Although this rule is not absolute, it is advisable to maintain the common tone whenever feasible. In going from one chord to the next, it is wise to keep the voices as close and compact as possible. In fact, the more fixed the better. Chords that leap up and down, giving a false impression of melodic interest, are weaker and invite faulty progression.

Ex. 24

(a) weak   better (b) weak   better (c) weak   better

tritone

at a) the G in the alto, instead of being retained, skips down a third. Moreover, the covered fifth between the soprano and tenor voice has a weakening effect.

at b) the C in the soprano, instead of being retained as a common tone, skips up a fourth.

at c) an exception is occasionally made as in the progression II to V, where it would be better to move the three upper parts downward as the bass skips up a fourth. This way the tritone feeling is less manifest.* (More on the tritone later.)

Root Progressions by Steps

When root progressions follow suit by steps, either up (as I to II, IV to V, etc.) or down (III to II, etc.), it is best to so place the voices that the highest tone (the soprano) moves by one step in contrary motion to the lowest tone (the bass).

Ex. 25

good   good   weak   good   good   weak

I   II   III   II

* Gioseffo Zarlino (1517–1590), an outstanding theorist of the sixteenth century and a pioneer in harmony, forbade the use of successive major thirds as shaping the TRITONE.

Aug. 4th

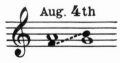

16

The progression V to VI is an exception. The leading tone moves up a degree, parallel with the bass, as the other two voices move downward necessitating the doubling of the third of the submediant (VI). (See deceptive progressions, P. 28)

Ex. 26

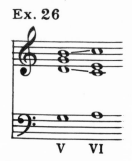

V   VI

It is possible to have three root progressions in succession by step, in either direction.

Ex. 27

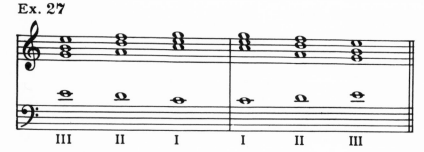

III   II   I   I   II   III

Crossing of Voices

Crossing of voices is not permissible in strict harmony. The C in the alto voice skips up to E, as the G in the soprano crosses down to the C below.

Ex. 28

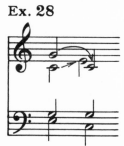

However, if the common tone rule is observed, voice crossings are not likely to occur in any of the harmony exercises.

4. Triads and Inversions of the Major Scale

Triads in Root Position

A TRIAD is in ROOT POSITION when the root (or fundamental) of the chord appears in the lowest part.

Ex. 28a

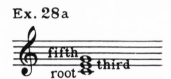

The tone most often doubled is the fundamental itself.

Below is an example of chords in root position, each with their fundamentals doubled.

Ex. 29

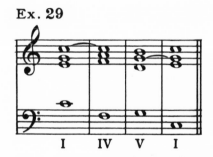

Bearing in mind the primary rules, the student is now prepared to write his first exercises in four-part harmony.

For the present all exercises are to be written in CLOSE POSITION, with the soprano, alto and tenor in the treble clef, and the bass alone, in the bass clef.

Unless otherwise specified (as pos. 3, or pos. 5), exercises are to begin in position of octave (pos. 8).

Ex. 30

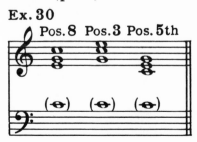

Note: Attention is called to the fact that in harmony the term *position* is used in three connotations. 1) OPEN position and CLOSE position signifies placement of chords. 2) position of 3rd, 5th and 8th indicates the position of the soprano, the highest voice. 3) and ROOT position signifies triads with the root in the bass.

Common tones should be indicated by a tie. (See Ex. 29.)

The range of an individual voice generally should not exceed an octave, the bass excepted, which may extend an octave and a fifth. Each chord, unless otherwise specified, is to have the metrical value of a whole note.

Exercises in Triads in Root Position

Employing triads on THREE different degrees.

I–IV–I–V–I in G major
          in B flat major

I–V–II–V–I in D major
          in A flat major pos. 5

I–IV–V–I   in G major
          in F major

I–VI–V–I   in C major
          in E major pos. 5

Employing triads on FOUR different degrees.

I–V–II–IV–V–I In D flat major
              in A major, pos. 3

I–IV–V–II–V–I in B flat major
              in E flat major, pos. 5

I–VI–II–V–I in G major
           in A flat major, pos. 3

Employing triads on FIVE different degrees.

I–IV–II–VI–IV–V–I in C major
                  in F sharp major, pos. 5

I–VI–IV–V–III–VI–IV–V–I in D major
                         in A flat major, pos. 5

I–VI–III–IV–V–I in D major
              in B flat major

Employing triads on six different degrees.

I–VI–II–III–I–IV–V–I in B flat major, pos. 5
in G major, pos. 5

Employing triads on each of the SEVEN degrees of the major scale.

The next exercise is based on a harmonic sequence. Any pattern of two or more chords imitated on successive intervals may be considered a sequence. Brackets indicate the pattern to be followed.

I– ⌐VI–II⌐ – ⌐VII–III⌐ – ⌐I–IV⌐ – ⌐II–V⌐ I. in F major
in A major.

Note: The diminished triad (here VII) is seldom used in root position, except, as in this instance, in the course of a sequence. Elaboration on sequences will occur later.

Symbols Used in Inversions

There is little justification for employing figured bass symbols today to indicate inversions. They are a relic of the time before Rameau demonstrated the laws on chords and their inversions, and are, therefore, a needless complication. We prefer, instead, to use the simpler alphabetical symbols, a, b, c and d, to indicate the four inversions in common usage. For example, Va = first inversion, IIIb = second inversion, etc. However, since most textbooks on harmony as well as counterpoint still employ figured bass symbols, the inversions of triads and seventh chords are listed below with their corresponding figured bass symbols.

Triads:
    root position   V   = V
    first inversion   Va = V6   chord of the sixth
    second inversion Vb = V6/4 chord of the fourth and sixth

Seventh Chords:
    root position   V7 = V7
    first inversion   V7a = V6/5 chord of the fifth and sixth
    second inversion Vb = V4/3 chord of the third and fourth
    third inversion   Vc = V2 chord of the second

Triads in First Inversion

In the first inversion of a triad the third is placed in the bass. The fifth is a third, and the root ·is a sixth above the bass. Known as the *chord of the sixth*, the figured bass symbol is designated by a 6 next to the Roman numeral.

Ex. 30a

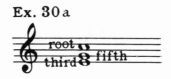

It is preferable to double the root in the first inversion of triads (at a), although doubling of the fifth (b), is almost as frequent. The third —the bass itself (c), is seldom doubled. The exception is the supertonic, which sounds best with the bass, the original third, doubled (See dim. II chord in minor, P. 32).

Ex. 31

(a) root doubled   (b) fifth doubled   (c) third doubled

Doubling the third in position of fifth should be avoided in all first inversion triads.

Ex. 32

Unisons are more frequently encountered in the first inversions of triads than in root position.

Ex. 33

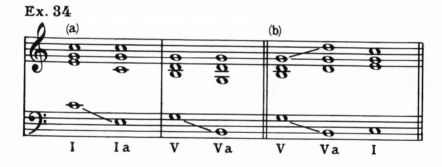

The skip of a sixth in the bass, from root position to first inversion (at a), is permissible. An exchange of the same chord may also take place in the three upper parts (b), an exception to the rule for common tones.

Ex. 34

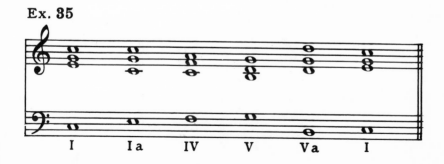

Illustration incorporating triads in first inversions.

Ex. 35

I–Ia–IV–IVa–V–Va–I in G major
in E flat major, pos.3
I–Ia–IV–II–V–Va–Ia–VI–IIa (third doubled)–V–I.
in B. maj.
in A flat maj. pos.5
I–VI–Ia (double fifth in unison)–IIa (double third)–V–Va–I.
in A maj.
in E flat maj.

Triads in Second Inversion

In the second inversion of a triad the fifth is in the bass. The root is a fourth, and the third is a sixth above the bass. Known as the chord of the fourth and sixth, a small letter b, next to the Roman numeral (like Ib, Vb, etc.), indicates the second inversion. The bass, the original fifth, is always doubled.

Ex. 35a

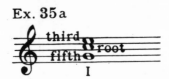

There are THREE principal species of second inversions, each one distinctly recognizable by its individual characteristics.

1. Cadential 6/4 Chord. The cadential 6/4 chord is the second inversion of the tonic, designated Ib, and occurs on a strongly *accented* beat.

Ex. 36

As its name suggests, it is most often used at cadence points at either phrase endings, or, at the end of a piece. The Ib chord commonly resolves immediately into the dominant (V), the bass being retained or skipping to the octave below. Some theorists refer to the progression Ib to V, as a delayed dominant chord. The third and the sixth above the bass being construed as a momentary displacement (or suspension) of the dominant. (See suspensions, page 58 .)

EXERCISE:

I—IV—Ib (cadential 6/4)—V—I. In G major

in E flat major, pos.3

2. Passing 6/4 Chord. The passing 6/4 chord is the second inversion of the dominant triad, designated Vb, and occurs on an *unaccented* beat. It is most often used like a passing tone (to be discussed later), connecting a triad to its first inversion (at a). In the passing Vb, however, the stepwise movement in the bass becomes a *consonant* (at b).

Ex. 37

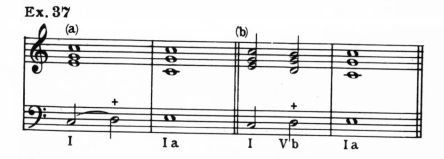

I   I a   I   V'b   I a

EXERCISE:

I—Vb (passing 6/4)—Ia—IV—II—V—I. in F major

in D major, pos.3

3. Plagal 6/4 Chord. The plagal 6/4 chord is the second inversion of subdominant triad, designated IVb. This chord has several unusual characteristics. It is one of the few chords that form a satisfactory cadence without need of the dominant (V) as the penultimate chord. It is preceded and followed by the tonic triad. Popularly known as the "hymn close" (Amen), the soprano and bass are repeated three times in the most effective position of this cadence. The three successive chords comprising the plagal cadence have *equal* stresses.

Ex. 38

I   IVb   I

EXERCISE:

I–VI–III–V–I–IVb–I (plagal cadence) in A major
                                      in F major

Review exercise, incorporating all three types of second inversions:

*I–Vb–Ia–IV–V–IVa–Ib**–IV–II–VIa–III–IIa–Ib–V–I–IVb–I.
                                       in E flat major
                                       in B major

* To avoid faulty progressions, this exercise must be carefully executed.
** In this exercise, Ib is also used as a passing 6/4 chord.

5. The Dominant Seventh Chord

The Dominant Seventh Chord and Its Inversions

WHEN A THIRD is placed over a triad, a chord of the SEVENTH is formed. Hence, seventh chords consist of *four different tones* a third apart. By far the most commonly used chord of the seventh is the one built on the fifth degree of the diatonic scale, known as the DOMINANT SEVENTH, or V7, chord. The complete chord consists of the major triad and minor seventh.

Ex. 39

It would be appropriate to name it the "natural dominant seventh" since it forms the necessary intervals of a dominant seventh without need of alteration. (See P. 85)

The dominant V7 chord was not formally recognized as an independent chord until the early part of the eighteenth century. Since that time it has been—and still remains—for all practical purposes, with the exception of the tonic triad, the most indispensable of all chords. To a great extent the independent use of the dominant seventh was responsible for the expansion and growth of classical structures.

With four tones available, three inversions are possible, in addition to the root position.

Ex. 40

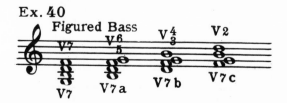

ROOT POSITION is designated V7. The FIRST INVERSION has the third in the bass and the fifth, seventh and root above it, and is designated V7a. The SECOND INVERSION has the fifth in the bass, and the seventh, root and third above it, and is designated V7b. The THIRD INVERSION has the seventh itself in the bass, and the root, third and fifth above it, and is designated V7c.

Wherever the seventh appears, it should resolve one degree downward into the tonic triad, its normal resolution.

Ex.41

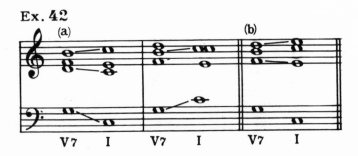

Note: In the third inversion the seventh, now in the bass, resolves into Ia.

In the progression V7 to I, a peculiar situation arises due to the presence of both the leading tone, which resolves a semitone up, and the minor seventh, which resolves one degree down.

Ex. 41 a

Therefore, in *root position,* when the V7 chord appears in its complete form, the fifth has to be omitted in the tonic resolution to avoid faulty progression. Hence, the fundamental of I is usually tripled (a). Although, if it resolves to pos.3, (b), the third is doubled.

Ex. 42

On the other hand, should the complete triad be desired in the tonic resolution, then the fundamental of V7 is doubled and the fifth omitted.

Ex. 43

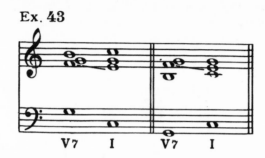

The fifth of V7 may be omitted in any of its inversions, when necessary, without loss of the dominant character.

Ex. 44

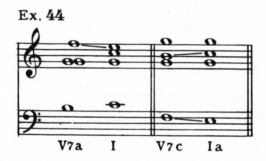

EXERCISES in root position:

I—IIa—Ib—V7—I in A major
  in B flat major, pos. 3
I—VI—IIa—V7 (omit fifth)—I in D major
  in E flat major pos. 3

EXERCISE in first inversion:

I—V7a—I—IV—Ib—V7—I in G major
  in A flat major

EXERCISE in second inversion:

I—V7b—I—V7a—I—V7—I in F sharp major
  in D flat major pos. 3

EXERCISE in third inversion:

I—V7c—Ia—IV—V7a—I—IVb—I in B major, pos. 3
  in F major, pos. 3

Dominant Seventh Chords (continued)

Besides the normal resolution, the V7 may take an unexpected or deceptive turn. The commonest of these is the deceptive progression V7 to VI. In this case the third of VI must be doubled.

Ex. 45

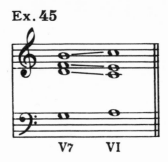

An exchange of the V7 chord to any of its inversions is permissible. The resolution then takes place according to its newly gained position.

Ex. 46

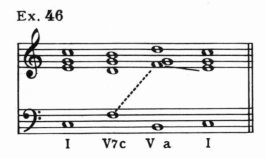

Other possible odd and unusual turns: V7c–IV–to Ia. The seventh, retained in the bass, first resolves into a subdominant consonance. The final resolution follows on Ia.

Ex. 47

In the next example V7c resolves into the mediant (III), instead of Ia.

Ex. 48

I   V7 c   III

This odd, yet entirely correct, progression, V7 to IVa, seems to require no resolution at all.

Ex: 49

V7   IV a

In another unusual turn, best seen in open position, the seventh *rises* one degree. The upward moving scale sequence in thirds tends to draw the seventh in opposition to the common resolution. It is also reminiscent of the progression I—Vb—to Ia, (P. 23) which connects the tonic triad to its first inversion.

Ex. 50

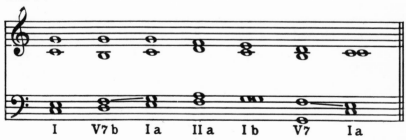

I   V7 b   I a   II a   I b   V7   I a

EXERCISE: combining the three inversions of the V7 chord.

I—V7—VI—IV—Ia—V7a—I—V7b—V7c—III—VI—IIa—Ib—V7—I.

in B flat maj.
in D maj.

6. Minor Modes and Scales

ALL MINOR SCALES are MODES, in a sense, as distinguished from keys which indicate tonality. This is so even though, like the melodic and harmonic minor scales, they have written signatures. To illustrate their ambiguity we need only take the C major scale, which, starting from A to the octave A above, forms the "natural" scale of A minor. But it is also equivalent to the descending melodic minor scale, and synonymous with the Greek AEOLIAN mode.

During the past century at least a dozen kinds of minor scales have come into use largely through the discovery (or rather re-discovery) of composer-folklorists. Broadly speaking, it can be said that any seventone scale extending from octave to octave and which contains the MINOR THIRD and PERFECT FIFTH, may be regarded as a form of minor scale.

The Melodic Minor and Harmonic Minor Scales

In our major-minor system, three kinds of minor scales have been in common use, the two species of melodic minor and the harmonic minor. Taking A minor (the relative minor of C major) as the basis, they are:

The MELODIC MINOR scale, which has two different forms, one ascending and one descending. Ascending, degrees VI and VII are chromatically raised a semitone. Descending, both the VII and VI are lowered a half-step.

Ex. 51

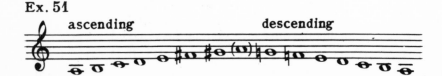

ascending   descending

The HARMONIC MINOR scale is diatonic, with the exception of the VIIth degree (the leading-tone) which is raised a chromatic half-step. The harmonic minor scale remains the same both ascending and descending. It is, therefore, the most constant of the three.

Ex. 52

In view of their obscure nature and to avoid needless confusion, the present study is confined to chords of the HARMONIC MINOR scale. (See Chapter 44.)

7. Triads and Inversions of the Harmonic Minor Scale

Triads in Root Position

Ex. 53

On I the triad is minor
On II the triad is diminished
On III the triad is augmented
On IV the triad is minor
On V the triad is major
On VI the triad is major
On VII the triad is diminished

The diminished II chord, like all diminished triads, is most effective in the first inversion with the bass (the original third) doubled, and in the position of the octave or third. Position of the fifth is best avoided.

Ex. 54

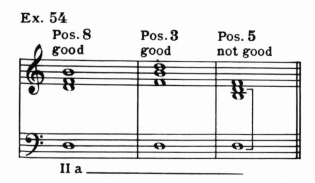

The IIa is best preceded by VI and commonly leads directly to the cadence.

Ex. 55

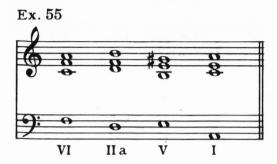

VI   II a   V   I

The augmented triad on III (like all augmented triads) has two good resolutions: to the major triad a perfect fifth below (at a), or to I, a minor third below (at b).

Ex. 56

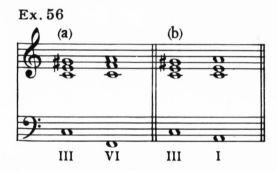

III   VI   III   I

Inversions

With the exception of IIa, the common rules for progressions and doublings already given for triads of the major scale and their inversions apply equally to the minor.

Illustration incorporating triads of the harmonic minor scale:

Ex. 57

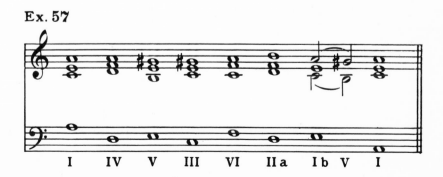

I   IV   V   III   VI   II a   I b   V   I

EXERCISES:

I–V–III–VI–IIa–Ib–V7–I in D minor

in B minor, pos. 3

I–V7–VI–IV–V–III–I in C minor

in E minor

EXERCISES in Inversions:

I–V7c–Ia–IV–V–V7b–I–IIIa–VI–IIa–Ib–V–I in C minor pos. 3

in A minor pos. 3

I–Ia–IV–V–V7a–I–VI–III–V7b–I–IIa–Ib–V7–I in C minor

in D minor

8. Secondary Seventh Chords

SECONDARY SEVENTH chords are seventh chords built on degrees of the scale other than the dominant. However, none of them have the same intervals as the V7 chord (major triad and minor seventh) which invests the dominant seventh with its unique character and function. To identify secondary sevenths, first name the kind of triad, then the kind of seventh above the fundamental. Thus, the seventh chord on I, in C major, consists of a major triad and a major seventh and is designated major-major (abbreviated, maj.maj.).

Ex. 57a

In A minor, the seventh chord on I, consists of a minor triad and a major seventh, and is designated min-maj.

Ex. 57b

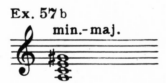

Secondary Seventh Chords of the Major Scale

Ex. 58

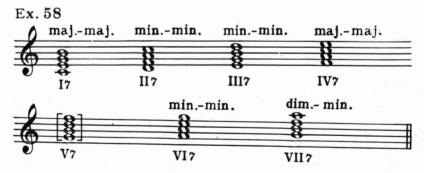

on I7 and IV7, major-major (maj-maj)
on II7, III7 and VI7, minor-minor (min-min)
and on VII7 diminished-minor (dim-min)

Secondary Seventh Chords of the Harmonic Minor Scale

Ex. 59

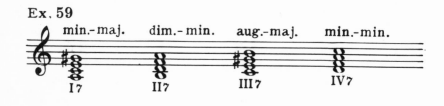

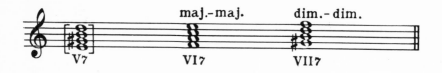

on I7, minor-major (min-maj)
on II7, diminished-minor (dim-min)
on III7, augmented-major (aug-maj)
on IV7, minor-minor (min-min)
on VI7, major-major (maj-maj)
and on VII7, diminished-diminished (dim-dim)

Notice that the harmonic minor scale contains seven *different* kinds of seventh chord, including the V7. The major scale has only four.

Their differences are more apparent when transposed to a common root, C.

Ex. 60

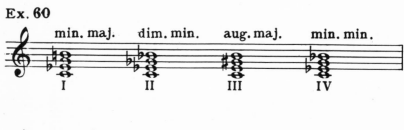

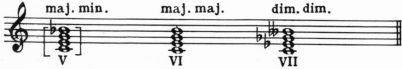

In secondary seventh chords, the seventh commonly resolves down one degree, like the V7. This also applies to all inversions of secondary seventh chords.

Ex. 61

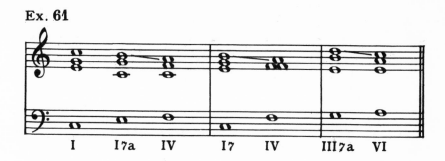

It may happen that the seventh is held over until the next chord.

An exception occurs when the seventh of I7, the leading tone (in either major or minor), resolves as an accented appogiatura by moving up a semitone, to the tonic.

Ex. 62

It may happen that the seventh is held over until the next chord. The resolution then occurs in the chord which follows:

Ex. 63

or, the seventh may be retained as a suspension. In either case it resolves one degree down into the next chord. (Appogiaturas, suspensions and other non-harmonic tones are discussed later.)

Ex. 64

EXERCISES in major combining secondary seventh chords:

I–IV–II7 (omit fifth)–I in G major
in A major

I–VI7–II7 (omit fifth)–V7–I in A flat major
in E major

I–VI7–II7b–VII7c–V7–I in F major
in B major

I–IV7–II7a–V7c–I7a–IV–VII7–V7a–I–IV7a–VII7c–V7–I
in C major
in G major, pos. 3

EXERCISES in harmonic minor:

I–I7a–VI (omit fifth)–IV7–V–I in A minor
in E minor

I–II!7–VI–II7a–II7b–V7–I in D minor, pos. 3
in F sharp minor

9. The Dominant Ninth Chord

The Dominant Ninth Chord and Its Inversions

WHEN A THIRD is placed over a seventh chord, a chord of the ninth is formed. This results in a chord consisting of five tones in its complete form.

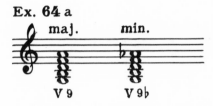

Ex. 64 a

The ninth chord on the fifth degree of the scale, like the V7, contains the natural intervals of the DOMINANT NINTH. It consists of the major third, perfect fifth, minor seventh and the major, or minor, ninth above the root, and is designated V9. In four-part writing one tone, commonly the fifth, is omitted.

Ex. 65

With five tones available, four inversions are possible in addition to the root position. The ninth, like the seventh, generally resolves one degree downward into the tonic triad. However, it resolves occasionally up a third, especially in the inversions. The use of the ninth in these chords necessitates a widening in distribution of the four voices. Therefore, it is advisable to demonstrate some of these examples in open position. The inversions of the V9 are designated: V9a, V9b, V9c and V9d.

EXERCISES: (in close position)

I—V9 (omit fifth)—I in G major

in F sharp minor, pos. 5

I—VI—IIa—V9 (omit fifth)—I in B major

in C minor, pos. 3

The first inversion, V9a

In the first inversion the THIRD is in the bass, and the fifth is omitted.

Ex. 66

Note: Exercises in the *inversions*, as shown above, may be executed in OPEN POSITION, with the soprano and alto in the treble clef. And the tenor and bass in the bass clef.

EXERCISES: (in open position)

I—V9a (omit fifth)—I in B flat major, pos. 5

in E minor, pos. 5

The second inversion, V9b

In the second inversion the FIFTH is in the bass.

Ex. 67

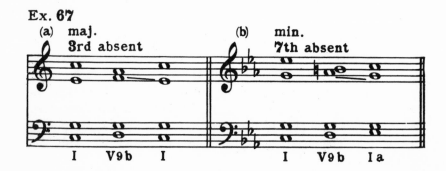

At 67a, the third is omitted. The seventh resolves one degree down, as usual, and the ninth rises a third, back to C, to prevent parallel fifths. At 67b, the seventh is absent and the minor ninth takes its place, resolving one degree down.

EXERCISES: (in open position)

I–V9b (omit third)–I–IV–Ib–V7–I in B major
                                            in C minor

I–V9b (omit seventh)–Ia–IIa–V–I in E flat major, pos. 3
                                        in C sharp minor, pos. 3

The third inversion, V9c

In the third inversion the SEVENTH is in the bass, and the fifth is absent. Both the seventh and the ninth resolve down one degree.

Ex. 68

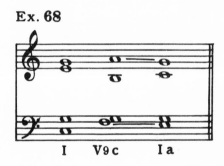

I   V9 c   I a

EXERCISE (in open position)

I–V9c (omit fifth)–Ia–V7b–I–V7–I in A major, pos. 5
                                      in G minor, pos. 5

The fourth inversion, V9d

Some theorists maintain there is no true fourth inversion of a ninth chord because the ninth must be nine (or sixteen) notes above the fundamental. However, if we accept the validity of seventh chords in their third inversions (where no actual seventh exists above its fundamental) then, by the same token, we must acknowledge the validity of ninth chords in their fourth inversions.

Therefore, in the fourth inversion the NINTH itself is in the bass. Although heard mostly in major, it can be effective in minor as well. The ninth may rise a third (Ex. 69),

Ex. 69

I   V9d   I   I   V9d   I

or resolve down one degree together with the seventh (Ex. 70).

Ex. 70

I   V9d   Ib   I   V9d   Ib

EXERCISES (in open position)

I–V9d–I in A major, pos. 5

        in E minor, pos. 5

I–V9d–Ib–V7–I in A major, pos. 3

              in D minor, pos. 3

(in close position)

I–VI–V9d–Ib–II7a–V–I in D major, pos. 3

                     in C minor, pos. 3

(in open position)

I–VI–II–V9d–Ib–V–I in A major, pos. 3

10. Dominant Eleventh and Thirteenth Chords

CHORDS OF THE V^{11} and V^{13} theoretically contain six and seven tones, respectively. In most instances the root, minor seventh or minor ninth, plus the eleventh or thirteenth—as the case may be—suffice to identify these chords. The choice of the fourth tone, in four-part writing, may be selected at one's discretion. Otherwise, these chords are to be treated in the same manner as V7 and V9 chords.

Shown in open or close position, below are a number of V^{11} and V^{13} chords commonly met with. The arabic numerals indicate which chord tones are employed.

Ex. 71

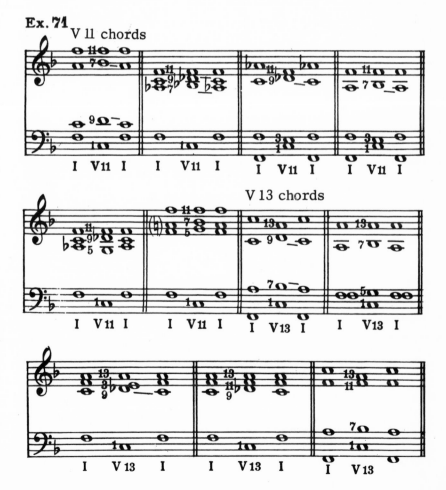

II. Secondary Ninth, Eleventh and Thirteenth Chords

ALTHOUGH 9th, 11th and 13th chords of NON-DOMINANT formation are occasionally mentioned, they have never been an organic or systematic part of harmony instruction. This is perplexing since harmony derived from the principle of thirds built over thirds. Yet, previous efforts by theorists to probe these chords have been discarded or were unsuccessful. Inasmuch as our objective here is to clarify traditional harmony, we will not delve now into these problems. (9th, 11th and 13th chords of non-dominant origin are discussed in Chapter 45.)

12. Sequences

Tonal and Real Sequences

A SEQUENCE IS the repetition of a melodic or harmonic phrase, or both, transposed to another interval. Sequences are most often a second apart. The phrase which is repeated (marked by brackets) is called the PATTERN. When the transposition is modified to conform with diatonic harmony it is a TONAL sequence.

Ex. 72

When the transposition is exact, it is a REAL sequence.

Ex. 73

Sequences in Alternating Seventh Chords and Triads

Secondary seventh chords are ideally suited to sequential treatment. A selected set of two or more chord progressions may form a sequence pattern, as shown in Example 74. At present only tonal (diatonic) sequences are considered.

Ex. 74

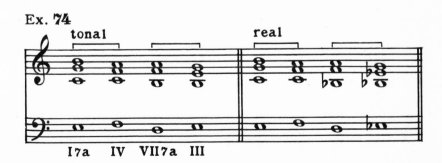

The following exercise is a tonal sequence with a two-chord pattern of alternating secondary sevenths resolving into triads.

EXERCISE:

⌐Pattern¬ ⌐Sequence¬ ⌐Sequence¬ ⌐Sequence¬
I– I7a–IV – VII7a–III   VI7a–II   V7a–I   in F sharp major
                                             in B major

Next, we present a two-bar sequence pattern (beginning at bar two) consisting of a triad and a seventh chord which then resolves into another seventh chord (bar three).

Ex. 75

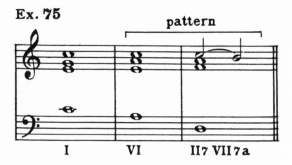

I   VI   II7 VII7a

EXERCISE: The student is to continue the pattern (indicated in brackets) to the end.

I–VI–(II7–VII7a) V–(I7–VI7a) IV–(VII7–II7a)–III–(VI7–IV7a)
II–(V7–III7a) I–(IV7–II7a) V7–I in D major
                                       in A major, pos. 5

Melody Accompanied by Successions of Resolving Seventh Chords

Commencing on a given tonic triad, a sequence pattern consisting of resolving sevenths alone can be interestingly continued almost indefinitely.

Ex. 76

To illustrate how such a device works, we expand the above sequence pattern into an accompaniment figure in 3/4 time. Each chord is to be repeated three times to the measure (as shown at Ex. 77).

Ex. 77

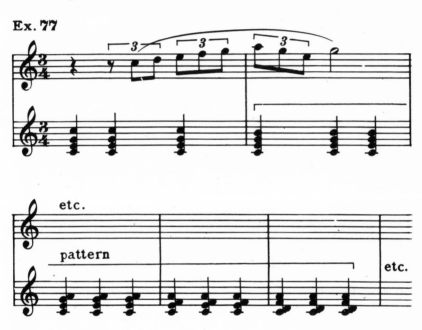

EXERCISE: Treating example 76 as a piano accompaniment, the student is then to compose a freely written melody in the upper staff—the first two measures are given—and continue to the end of the sequence series. The melody itself, however, though remaining diatonic, should NOT be sequential.

Note: The melody constitutes an added *fifth* voice to the four-part harmony below it. Hence, being independent of the harmonic scheme, the melody need not conform strictly with harmony rules. (See P.   )

Other metrical figures may be devised using Example 76 for the pattern. For instance: in 6/8 time, it is now changed to an accompaniment figure of broken chords, an octave lower.

Ex. 78

EXERCISE: Following the above new metrical pattern, continue to the end as before.

Below is an example in 2/4 meter. The harmonic pattern is now in the upper staff, and the melody is below it.

Ex. 79

EXERCISE: Continue melody as before.

Composers from BACH to STRAVINSKY have availed themselves of similar sequential harmonic devices. (More of sequences later.)

PART ONE

DIATONIC PROCESSES

Section Two

13. Diatonic Modulation

Introduction

WE HAVE STATED from the beginning that harmony ought to be learned as a separate entity, apart from melodic considerations. This holds true especially for modulatory procedures. To demonstrate modulations with compositional examples, as is generally the case, is to become further entangled with factors of rhythm, timing, motivic involvement, tensions and other components which belong to the realm of composition. Consequently, the primary consideration in the exposition of modulation continues to be harmonic, rather than melodic or contrapuntal, progressions.

True modulation in the classical sense signifies a change from one key to another, normally for the purpose of remaining for some time in the new key. Modulations may be DIATONIC, CHROMATIC or ENHARMONIC.

Diatonic Modulation Defined

It is a curious fact that Diatonic Modulation is the only *absolute* modulation. Yet, paradoxically, it has been relegated to the forgotten techniques. It is a pity, for the study of diatonic modulation tends to prove, more than any other element of harmonic study, that the "logistics" of harmony did not come about through chance.

The question arises: how can modulations to distant keys be accomplished by diatonic processes when at least one chromatic change is required to modulate even to the closest related key?

Diatonic modulation takes place when chords are so arranged that each accidental, whether sharp or flat, must first be rendered diatonic by *implication* before it can be used. That is to say, each (chromatic) change has to be diatonically prepared, step by step.

For example: to modulate from C major to a key having sharps, the two triads which tend to lead toward a sharp key—yet remaining indigenous to C—are either G major or E minor. Thus, if we select E minor, the implied signature of which contains one sharp (F sharp), it can then be followed by B minor, since the F sharp of the B minor triad has been diatonically prepared.

Ex. 80 (1) (2) (3)

The C chord (1) has no sharps or flats. The E minor chord (2), although indigenous to C, *implies* one sharp. Hence, the F sharp contained in B minor (3), has become diatonic.

Similarly, if the objective is to modulate from C major to a flat key, a triad must be used whose implied signature (not key) would contain one flat—either the D minor or F major triad. Choosing F major, the B flat major chord may then follow, since it has been rendered diatonic, etc.

Ex. 81 (1) (2) (3)

By employing the above method of gradual subtraction or addition, as warranted by the circumstances, a species of modulation occurs—it will be demonstrated—before any DOMINANT CHORD comes into consideration. Only after the modulation proper has been effected (to be marked "X"), may the dominant chord of the new key be used to complete the cadence. Thus, it will be shown that diatonic modulation can be accomplished *solely by means of triads in root position*.

Table of Root Progressions

In the process of making modulations the student naturally has to rely on his own resources for the choice of chords and chord progressions. In addition, he must keep constant control of his modulatory moves. Therefore, before going into modulation proper, we have to consider several other factors essential to a comprehensive knowledge of harmonization, and indispensable in executing smooth and convincing modulations. To assist him, we present below a table of root progressions commonly used, to serve as a guide in functional moves. It has been my experience that this method is simpler yet far more effective than the indirect way of tabulating those chords which best *precede* and *follow* one another.

Most frequently used root progressions are:

Ex. 82

up a fourth   up a fifth   down a third

Less frequently used root progressions are:

Ex. 83

up a third up a step   down a step

Too many similar moves in the bass, moreover, even though harmonically correct, become tedious and should be avoided.

Ex. 84

14. Diatonic Modulation (Continued)

Directions for Executing Diatonic Modulation

ROOT TRIADS should be exclusively employed until the chord common to the new key has been reached. This chord (to be marked Chord "X") signifies that the *modulation proper* has been accomplished; at this point, only a cadence is lacking to complete the modulation. (Cadences will be discussed later.)

Although no chord is to be repeated, the immediate repetition or shifting of the same chord (for melodic or rhythmic reasons) is not only permissible, but occasionally advantageous. (See Ex. 103.)

Avoid too many bass moves in the same direction. The ideal diatonic modulation should have a smooth, easily singable bass line.

Roman numerals are to be used at two places only: 1) on the first chord which represents the tonic (I) chord of the key about to be quitted, and 2) at chord "X," where the numeral should signify the chord's relation to the new key, and from there to the end of the modulation. Hence, chord "X" represents the beginning of the new key.

Chords appearing between the first chord and chord "X"—a sort of no-man's land—are to be considered as potential or implied *signatures* and not as *keys* (i.e., two flats or three sharps—never the key of B flat major or F sharp minor).

Note: Despite common usage, key and signature are not always synonymous. The original purpose of a signature was to prevent the overuse of accidentals. Therefore, a piece could be in the key of G minor, but if the note E natural occurs more frequently than E flat, it is simpler to designate one flat as the signature, although the key remains in G minor. This procedure was already used by Bach and other earlier composers, as well as by twentieth century composers.

The Importance of Balance Chords

Defined in simple terms, when a major triad is followed by its relative minor or vice-versa, the second chord becomes the BALANCE CHORD. For example, an E minor triad preceded by G major functions as a balance chord, both having the implied signature of one sharp.

Ex. 85

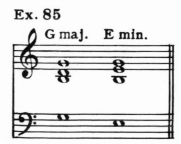

An E flat major triad serves likewise as the balance chord of the C minor triad.

Ex. 86

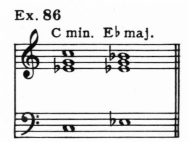

Thus, actually the balance chord makes no advance towards the key of destination. Rather, the purpose of this exchange is to achieve smoother chordal progressions and to avoid monotony. A well chosen BALANCE CHORD supplies the added artistic element to what otherwise would be mere mathematically calculated progressions.

EXERCISE:

Name the balance chord for E major
Name the balance chord for F minor
Name the balance chord for D flat minor
Name the balance chord for B minor

15. Diatonic Modulation up to Chord "X"

THE TERM CHORD "X," previously mentioned, signifies any triad contained in the diatonic scale of the new key with the exception of the I (tonic) chord and the V (dominant) chord of the new key. These two chords must be reserved for the cadence. Thus CHORD "X" acts as the pivotal or penultimate chord which prepares the cadence that will complete the modulation in the new key.

The following illustrates a diatonic modulation from C major to chord "X" of F sharp major (in this case, chord "X" is B major) mechanically made without using balance chords.

Ex. 87

As the triads progress from C major (the starting key) to chord "X" of F sharp major, one sharp is hypothetically added to each subsequent chord (by implication of its particular scale). Thus, the G triad implies the signature of one sharp, the D triad implies two sharps, A three sharps, E four sharps, and B five sharps. B is the subdominant (IV) chord of F sharp major, and is therefore chord "X." Notice, that although the above is theoretically correct, the bass line (consisting entirely of skips of fifths and fourths) is monotonous.

On the other hand, let us observe these modulatory progressions to chord "X," when interspersed with two judiciously selected *balance chords.*

Ex. 88

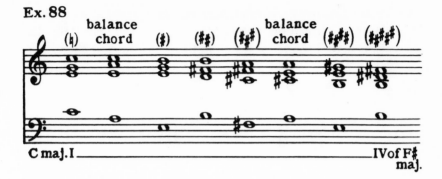

Now the mechanical feeling is avoided. The progressions are smoother and the bass moves are more natural. But important as balance chords are, they should not be employed casually. One or two of them carefully chosen will suffice, except in distant modulations, where as many as three balance chords may be required.

Since no chord should be repeated in a modulation, and since chord "X" can be neither I nor V of the new key, one of the four remaining chords, II, III, IV, or VI (or one of their derivatives II7, or IV7) will lead to the cadence.

Needless to say, strict harmony rules must be adhered to, as before.

EXERCISES: (for making modulations up to chord "X")

Major to major.
    Starting in C major, modulate to chord "X" of A flat major
    Starting in F sharp major, modulate to chord "X" of A major
    Starting in A major, modulate to chord "X" of F major
    Starting in E flat major, modulate to chord "X" of C major
    Starting in G major, modulate to chord "X" of B flat major

Minor to major.
    Starting in F minor, modulate to chord "X" of G major
    Starting in B minor, modulate to chord "X" of E flat major
    Starting in D minor, modulate to chord "X" of D major

Major to minor.
    Starting in C major, modulate to chord "X" of F sharp minor
    Starting in F major, modulate to chord "X" of B flat minor

Minor to minor.
    Starting in C minor, modulate to chord "X" of A minor
    Starting in D minor, modulate to chord "X" of F sharp minor

One final check will assure that the modulatory progressions to chord "X" have been diatonically accomplished. Each move must tally diatonically, first with the chord before it, then with the next chord.

Ex. 89

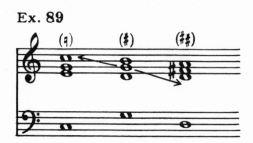

G, the second chord, is diatonic to C, the triad which precedes it. The G major triad also implies ONE SHARP. Hence, the F sharp contained in the D major triad, which follows, has been diatonically converted.

Up until now it has been shown that diatonic modulations to chord "X" can be manipulated solely by means of triads and that, contrary to common practice, modulations may be made from one key to another without resorting to the use of DOMINANT (V7) CHORDS. Melodic adornments and rhythmic considerations have been purposely omitted so that, first, the basic elements of diatonic modulation might be clearly observed. However, two other facets, NONHARMONIC TONES and CADENCES, have yet to be considered before demonstrating complete modulations.

16. Nonharmonic Tones

IN THE FINAL analysis all music within the scope of harmony consists of combinations of harmony tones (tones CONSONANT to the harmony), and nonharmonic tones (tones DISSONANT to the harmony).* The use of so-called non-harmonic tones can provide additional melodic and rhythmic interest to the individual voices. It is recommended, therefore, that a careful study be made of the various kinds of embellishments. A thorough knowledge of nonharmonic tones and their application is essential to understanding composition and counterpoint as well as harmony.

Passing Tones, Suspensions, Anticipations and Other Auxiliary Tones

1) PASSING TONES are tones dissonant to the harmony, progressing by step and used to connect two consonant chords. They usually occur on a weak beat, and may be single (a) or, combined (b).

Ex. 90

---

* "The European chain of thirds brought our Western music into other ways than those of the fourth-based music of the East . . . They barred the development of actual melody in the Oriental sense and led instead to the typical Western melody, which has essentially been harmony broken up (by) and cemented with passing notes." Curt Sachs, *The Rise of Music in The Ancient World*, p. 312.

2) Suspensions are tones held over or delayed while the rest of the chord changes. They may be unaccented (a) or (b) accented, (also called appogiaturas). An upward moving suspension (c) occasionally occurs in the leading tone.

Ex. 91

3) Anticipation is the opposite of suspension. One tone or more of the next chord are heard in advance—hence, in anticipation of the rest of the chord.

Ex. 92

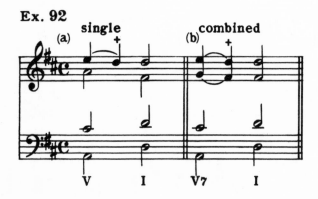

The D in the soprano (at a) and both the D in the soprano and the F sharp in the alto (at b) anticipate the resolution into D major. Suspensions and anticipations frequently appear together.

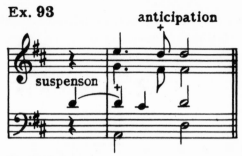

Ex. 93   anticipation   suspenson

Other Ornamentations

4) RETURNING MOTION (also called auxiliary tones) occurs when a tone reaches above or below by a step or half-step and immediately returns. Like other appogiaturas, it may be used singly or in combination.

Ex. 94 single   combined   single

Ex. 95   (combinations of passing tones and returning motion).

5) ÉCHAPPÉE is a tone which proceeds by step to a foreign tone before returning, by skip, to the next harmony tone.

Ex. 96

6) CAMBIATA is a tone that skips to a foreign tone before returning
by step to the next harmony tone.

Ex. 97

Two more species of nonharmonic tones are worth mentioning, even
though not directly connected with basic chordal progressions. The
first is ORGAN POINT (also called pedal point). This consists of a tone
sustained most often in the bass, on the tonic or dominant, while the
other parts move freely in changing harmonies above it (at 98a).

Ex. 98

(d) **Beethoven - Piano Sonata op.31 no.2**

Adagio

(L. H. Simplified)

etc.

A pedal point occurs less frequently in an upper voice (b) or in the middle part (c), or it may extend both below and above the moving parts (d).

Occasionally a double organpoint also may occur.

Ex. 99

The *second specie*, NONHARMONIC CHORDS, concerns the use of chords passing in opposite motion to the bass, both parts proceeding scalewise.

Ex. 100

These progressions operate much like passing tones, using passing chords instead. The dissonant chords are permissible so long as they progress by step from consonance to consonance.

Note: For those seeking a more thorough study of non-harmonic tones in four-part writing (chromatic as well as diatonic) no finer examples can be found than in the chorales of BACH.

17. Cadences

BESIDES THE use of embellishments, it is essential for the student to attain skill in first approaching and then making CADENCES, before attempting complete modulations. The closing chords most frequently employed in cadences are the progressions V (or V7) to I; or, the cadential close, Ib–V to I. Consequently, the chord of prime importance is the one which precedes the V–I, or, the cadential close. This is commonly either the SUPERTONIC in the first inversion (Ex. 101a), the SUBDOMINANT (101b); or one of its derivatives II7 (101c) and IV7 (101d). An exception is the plagal cadence, I–IVb–I (101e), which by-passes the use of the dominant.

Ex. 101

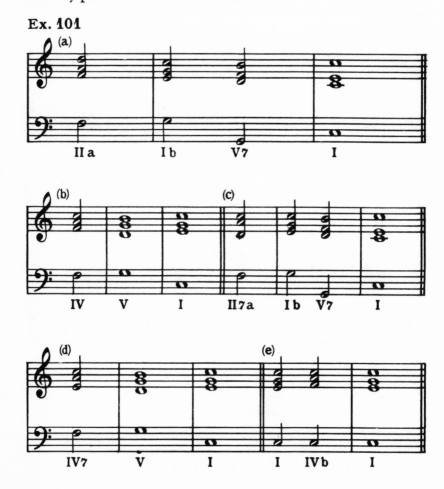

The cadences shown above are applicable in minor as well as in major.

Although classical cadence forms are limited, when rhythmic and melodic embellishments are added many variants are possible.

Below are two cadences with embellishments, one in major (at a) and one in minor (at b).

Ex. 102

EXERCISES: Construct cadences with embellishments added.

    IIa—Ib—V7—I in E major, 4/4 meter
    IVa—Ib—V7—I in F major, 3/4 meter
    II7b—Ib—V—I in G major, 4/4 meter
    II7a—V7—I—IVb—I in A minor, 3/4 meter
    IIa—Ib—V7—I in C minor, 6/8 meter
    IV7—Ib—V7—I in E minor, 4/4 meter

All cadences should terminate in the position of octave.

18. The Complete Diatonic Modulation

Final Reminders for Making Complete Modulations

FIRST TAKE THE modulation to chord "X," then add the cadence. Lastly, include rhythmic and melodic embellishments to suit.

Check each voice for parallel octaves and fifths. Remember, embellishments do not excuse faulty progressions, so use them sparingly. One or two well-chosen nonharmonic tones are more effective than profusely decorated exercises.

It is worth noting too, that in exercises in close position, nonharmonic tones are more frequent in the soprano and the bass than in the middle voices.

Besides the use of embellishments, interest may be heightened by the occasional rhythmic repetition of a chord. Striking the same chord twice in succession—or even three times—for melodic and rhythmic effect does not constitute an actual repetition (Ex. 103a), nor does skipping to another position of the same chord (Ex. 103b).

Ex. 103

Use only triads in root position to chord "X." However, inversions may be freely employed at the cadences.

Example 104 illustrates a diatonic modulation from C, to A major, consisting of triads alone, complete with cadence.

Ex. 104

Example 105 shows the identical modulation with embellishments (listed below) added.

Ex. 105

1. returning motion in soprano
2. suspension in soprano
3. returning motion in bass
4. appogiatura in tenor
5. passing tone in bass
6. returning motion in soprano
7. cambiata in soprano
8. anticipation in soprano
9. passing V7 in alto and tenor
10. appogiatura in tenor

19. Modulation to Remote Keys

THE EXAMPLES which follow include many kinds of diatonic modulation to distant keys. These should be carefully studied and assimilated by the student before he attempts his own complete modulations with embellishments and cadences.

Ex. 106 (sharps to flats)

Example 106, B major to F major, is divided into three segments: a) establishment of the starting key, b) modulation to chord "X," and c) cadence in the new key.

Ex. 107 (flats to sharps)

The above example, B flat to D major, shows how repeated chords add rhythmic and melodic strength to a modulation. Note: Up to chord "X" no other embellishments are employed.

Ex. 108

This modulation, from E major to E minor, stresses the importance of the diminished IIa in aiming at minor cadences. Note at bar five the use of the III chord in the lowered melodic minor form. It is one of the most effective approaches to the IIa in minor cadences.

Ex. 109

In the above example, B minor to G minor, notice the illusory parallel fifths between the soprano and the tenor near the end of the cadence. They are, however, consecutive fifths in appearance only. The G in the soprano is an anticipation, and without harmonic connotation.

Ex. 110

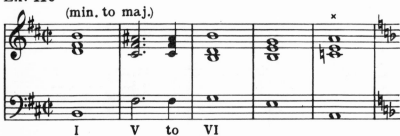

This is a very unusual diatonic modulation. The first three chords establish the original key, B minor, by means of the deceptive progression V—to VI. Thus we have a condition where a chord implying six sharps (F sharp major) may be logically followed by G (implying only one sharp), since G is indigenous to the starting chord, B minor. The G major triad is then followed by its balance chord, E minor, and one more progression brings it to chord "X" and the cadence.

The foregoing examples have included most types of diatonic modulation distantly related.

EXERCISES: for modulating to distant keys.

Modulate from A major to E flat major, pos. 3
Modulate from A major to B major to B minor, pos. 5
Modulate from A major to B flat major to B major
Modulate from A major to C sharp minor to C minor

After completing the above modulations, embellishments may be added.

20. Modulation to Related Keys

AN EFFECTIVE diatonic modulation to a related key is more difficult to accomplish than to a distant key, since the number of chords available —without repetition—narrows down to four diatonic chords, the II, III, IV and VI. Such modulations, therefore, are dependent upon artful manipulation of embellishments combined with skilful rhythmic timing.

However, if both the triads II and IV have been employed (as may be the case), then the II7 or IV7 may be substituted in leading to the cadence.

Ex. 111

The starting chord and key, C, unavoidably reappears as the V7 at the cadence.

Ex. 112

Since both the II (A minor) and IV (C major) of G major had to be used, the A-minor reappears as the II7, in leading to the cadence.

Ex. 113

(C maj. to A min.)

Ex. 114

(E min. to C maj.)

Examples 113 and 114 have no repeated chords.

Ex. 115

(A min. to D min.)

In the above modulation the tonality of A minor is first established by inserting the augmented triad (III of A minor) before progressing to the F major triad. Notice, though, that the G natural (dim. IIa) which follows the G sharp, with but one chord intervening—the F major triad—does not upset its diatonic flavor.

EXERCISES:

Modulate from D minor, to B flat major, pos. 3
Modulate from D major, to G major, pos. 5
Modulate from E minor, to A minor, pos. 8

To demonstrate that several varieties of the same modulation are possible, two totally different versions of a modulation from C major to C sharp minor are presented.

Ex. 116

21. Modulation in Open Position

IT MAY BE asked why the illustrations and exercises used throughout most of this treatise are given in close position rather than in open position, the more conventional manner of four-part writing. Through the experiences gathered over a quarter of a century of reviewing harmony with professional composers, conductors and orchestrators, it was discovered that the student is more secure, learns more quickly, and is better able to retain knowledge of fundamental harmonies and chord progressions when the bass is isolated from the three other voices. And as the student advances to more involved problems in harmony, the advantages of keeping close watch of the bass moves become increasingly apparent. This is especially true when keeping track of modulations.

Harmony as practiced today is a far cry from the earlier vocal conception, when music consisted chiefly of choral works. Harmony serves as the backbone of instrumental writing, from unpretentious songs with piano accompaniment, to symphonies of large dimensions. Practical application has shown, moreover, that one who has mastered harmony while working in *close position* encounters little if any difficulty in adjusting himself to writing in *open position*.

Below are two illustrations of diatonic modulations written in open position.

Ex. 117 (a)

(B maj. to C maj.)

Ex. 117 (b)
(C maj. to F# maj.)

EXERCISES: (Modulations in open position)

Modulate from D major to C major, pos. 3
Modulate from A major to E minor, pos. 5
Modulate from G major to C minor, pos. 8

For further practice in modulations in open position, any of the exercises previously given for close position may be utilized.

Resume of Part One

CONSECUTIVE FIFTHS and OCTAVES are to be avoided.

COMMON TONES should be held over wherever possible. When there is no common tone, as in stepwise progressions, the soprano and bass should move in contrary motion by step.

Inversions of triads present no problem, with the exception of the SUPERTONIC in minor. The IIa chord, usually avoided because of the TRITONE, is actually the perfect chord for approaching minor cadences.

The tendency of all seventh chords, DOMINANT and SECONDARY, to resolve one degree down was noted. Attention was focused on sequences and the interesting chain of harmonic progressions created by successions of resolving sevenths.

It was remarked that studies in traditional harmony eschew organic exploration of NINTH, ELEVENTH and THIRTEENTH CHORDS, other than DOMINANTS.

NONHARMONIC TONES were demonstrated as employed to embellish and enrich harmony exercises, albeit never as an excuse for faulty progressions.

DIATONIC MODULATION: in making modulations to all keys without resorting to the use of DOMINANTS, the student learns to understand the only *absolute* technique of modulation. He acquires skill in the smooth handling of chords and chord progressions under severe disciplinary conditions. And what is most important, the student learns to appreciate the meaning of functional DIATONIC ROOTS, the basis of our major-minor system. Therein ultimately lies the key to understanding the free use of ALL HARMONIES.

There are THIRTEEN DIATONIC CHORDS in harmony whose function exemplifies most chordal progressions encountered in classical music. These are: The FOUR TRIADS (major, minor, diminished and augmented), the SEVEN species of SEVENTH CHORDS (see Ex. 59), and the DOMINANT MAJOR and MINOR NINTH (V9) chords. Most other chords either stem from or are built over these thirteen basic chords.

"No single individual is capable of exhausting a subject
as profound as music. It is almost impossible for him not
to be constantly overlooking something."

J. P. Rameau (*Traité de l'harmonie*)

PART TWO

CHROMATIC PROCESSES

22. Chromatic Processes

ANY TONE OTHER than the seven tones of the major scale is, precisely
defined, a CHROMATIC TONE. Tones separated by a half-step written on
the same degree are chromatic, as for example, C to C sharp, D to D
flat, etc. In compositional practice harmonic progressions which contain a profusion of chromatic tones are referred to as CHROMATIC MUSIC,
a term especially applicable to the music of WAGNER and of late romantic composers, REGER, STRAUSS, MAHLER and BRUCKNER, etc.

The CHROMATIC SCALE emerged from, and was indeed considered
an extension of, the DIATONIC SCALE. It should be borne in mind that
classical composers were well aware of these inter-relationships and
conceived all chromatic harmonic progressions as resolving back to
their diatonic component. Our method of analyzing the chromatic
scale and its chord functions follows this classical precept.

Diatonic and Chromatic Half-steps

There are two ways of notating successive tones a half-step apart.
Semitone progressions written on two different degrees are DIATONIC
half-steps (at a).

Ex. 118

Semitone progressions written on the same degree are CHROMATIC half-steps (at b).

The major scale thus consists of five whole steps and two DIATONIC half-steps.

Ex. 119

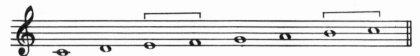

The Chromatic Scale

To construct the chromatic scale, five CHROMATIC SEMITONES are inserted between the seven tones of the major scale. Hence, the twelve tones of the complete chromatic scale consist of *five* whole steps, *two* diatonic half-steps and *five* chromatic half-steps. Most harmony books organize the ascending scale by chromatically raising all the five whole tones, and the descending scale by chromatically flatting them. From the viewpoint of the science of harmony, this procedure is incorrect. The chromatic scale should properly read as follows:

ascending

Ex. 120

Instead of raising the submediant, A to A sharp, the leading tone, B, is lowered to B flat.

descending

Ex. 121

Instead of lowering the dominant, G to G flat, the subdominant F is raised to F sharp.

23. The Tritone

The Tritone on the Ascending Chromatic Scale

ON THE ASCENDING chromatic scale each raised tone may be interpreted as a LEADING TONE, resolving into the diatonic triad a semitone above. This works out well on each chromatically raised degree with the exception of the submediant (VI). The A, when chromatically raised to A sharp, resolves naturally into the diminished triad on B, a TRITONE and a dissonant chord.

Ex. 122

tritone   concord

I   II   III   IV   V   VI   VII

In order that the A sharp may resolve into a consonant chord, the third, C, must also be raised a semitone to C sharp, thus compelling a resolution into B minor, a foreign key. Figuratively speaking, it "jumps the track."

Ex. 123

Therefore, instead of raising A to A sharp, the leading tone, B, should be flatted.

Ex. 124

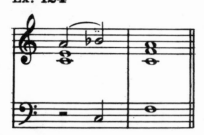

The lowered VII may now be interpreted as a V7 chord which resolves—in reverse—into F major, a consonant chord. In this way the diatonic relationship remains intact.

The Tritone on the Descending Chromatic Scale

On the DESCENDING chromatic scale each lowered tone, except one, may resolve into the diatonic consonant chord a semitone below. Now, however, a harmonic conflict arises between degrees V and IV. The G, when chromatically lowered to G flat, resolves into the SAME TRITONE—diminished triad on B—as in the ascending scale.

Ex. 125

To avoid the tritone this time, the E, as well as the G, has to be chromatically lowered a semitone, thus again forcing the resolution into a foreign key, now D flat major.

Ex. 126

Therefore, instead of lowering G to G flat, the F should be raised to F sharp. The raised IV may now be interpreted as a V7 chord which resolves—in reverse—into the consonant chord, G major. Again the diatonic tonality is preserved.

Ex. 127

In the ascending and descending chromatic scales the familiar troublemaker, the TRITONE, causes a harmonic conflict. Although much has been written about it, little light has been shed on the peculiarity of this obstacle. Future investigation may point to the tritone as the key to the solution of the question: does the nature of the 12-tone scale permit each tone to be harmonically independent? (See chapter 39). Once the problematic tritone is out of the way, all other chromatically altered tones and chords may be easily accounted for.

24. Cross-Relation

SOMETIMES A chromatic alteration occurs which causes a cross-relation.

Ex. 128

A cross-relation is the harmonic contradiction arising from the progression of a chromatic half-step which appears not in the same, but in a different voice. In strict harmony such a progression is considered faulty.

Ex. 129

When employed intentionally in a composition, these progressions can be quite effective. In twentieth century music cross-relations have become a favorite device.

Ex. 130

But they were by no means unknown in early contrapuntal music.

Ex. 131   Carlo Gesualdo (1560–1611)   J.S.Bach

25. Chromatically Altered Chords

Chromatically Altered Triads

MAJOR TRIADS may be altered into MINOR TRIADS, and commonly resolve into a chord a perfect fifth higher.

Ex. 132

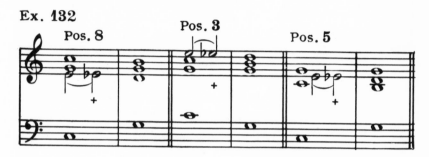

MINOR TRIADS may be chromatically altered into MAJOR TRIADS, and
commonly resolve into a chord a perfect fourth higher.

Ex. 133

DIMINISHED triads may be altered into MINOR (a) or MAJOR (b)
triads, and commonly resolve into a chord a perfect fifth lower.

Ex. 134

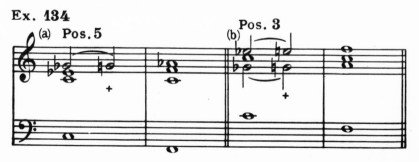

MAJOR and MINOR triads may be altered into AUGMENTED triads. AUGMENTED triads have two good resolutions, into a chord a perfect fifth (a), or a minor third (b) lower.

Ex. 135

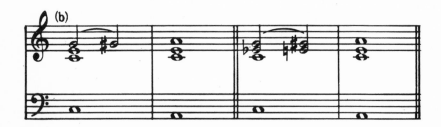

Note: Chromatic alterations should take place within the measure in the same manner as passing tones and other nonharmonic tones.

EXERCISES:

Alter F major to minor, and resolve
Alter B minor to major, and resolve pos. 3
Alter A minor to major, and resolve pos. 5
Alter D diminished to minor, and resolve
Alter A diminished to major, and resolve pos. 3
Alter E major to augmented, and resolve both ways, pos. 5
Alter F sharp minor to augmented, and resolve both ways

26. Chords Altered into Dominants

CHORDS ALTERED into dominants were a prominent harmonic idiosyncrasy in romantic music. These chords have survived and are today still a mainstay—a "cliché" of popular music. An objectionable feature lies in the mistaken notion that these chords may be interpreted variously as the dominant of a new key. Diatonic modulation proves this conception to be delusive. However, this does not entirely preclude modulation by means of altered dominants. But normally they function mainly as harmonic coloration, not as modulation.

Though few are aware of it, in BACH's time the dominant seventh chord was not considered an independent chord. In fact, it did not come into common usage until later in the eighteenth century.

Triads Altered Into V7 Chords

The distinction between the V7 chord on the FIFTH DEGREE and all other dominants accomplished by alterations—sometimes called secondary dominants—must be clearly differentiated.

Ex. 136

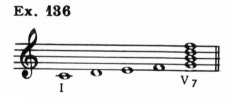

A triad on any degree of the scale may be converted into a dominant seventh chord by chromatic alteration. Thus in C major, the tonic triad may be so converted by simply adding the minor seventh, B flat.

Ex. 137

Chords altered into dominants commonly resolve into the triad a perfect fifth lower, like the diatonic V7.

Ex. 138

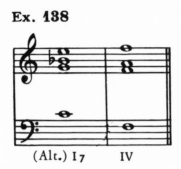

(Alt.) I 7   IV

This procedure can be followed on each degree of the scale, with the exception of the subdominant (IV), without abandoning the tonality. On IV, due to the tritone, the diatonic resolution is obstructed.

Ex. 139   (Shaded notes show resolution out of key.)

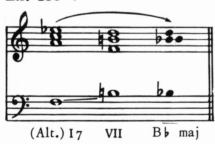

(Alt.) I 7   VII   B♭ maj

Since our objective is to show that chords altered into dominants rarely have modulatory significance, the subdominant (IV) is excluded from the exercises. (The diatonic V7 has been previously treated.)

Shown below are dominant sevenths on each degree of the scale and their diatonic resolutions.

Ex. 140

I altered into a V7 chord resolves into IV
II altered into a V7 chord resolves into V
III altered into a V7 chord resolves into VI
VI altered into a V7 chord resolves into II
VII altered into a V7 chord resolves into III

Directions for Altering Chords Into Dominants

Exercises are to commence and end with the tonic triad. FIRST, lead up to the degree to be altered into a V7 (to be marked "X"). SECOND, resolve into the triad a perfect fifth below (or fourth above). THIRD, continue on, and insert such chords as needed to complete the cadence in the original key. Alterations are best made within the same bar, as with altered triads.

Ex. 141

Only triads are to be used in leading to the chord to be altered. However, both CHROMATIC as well as DIATONIC embellishments may now be added.

One example of each of the five degrees to be altered follows (the point of alteration is indicated by an +):

Ex. 142 (I altered into a V7)

The triad on I, naturally, needs no preparation.

Ex. 143   (II altered into V7)

The altered II is best preceded by either VI or IV.

Ex. 144   (III altered into a V7)

The altered III is best preceded by I or VI.

Ex. 145 (VI altered into a V7)

VI Alt.VI 7

Note: The degrees IV7 and V7 are omitted for reasons previously explained.

The alteredVI7 is best preceded by I or III.

VII Altered Into a V7 Chord

The diminished triad on VII is the only degree which requires a double alteration in order to convert it into a V7 chord. Both the THIRD and FIFTH have to be chromatically raised. Therefore, the altered VII7 requires special preparation. In its complete form it should be preceded by VI in position of 5.

Ex. 146

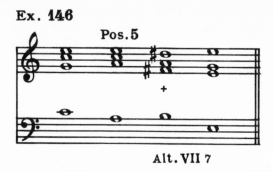

Alt. VII 7

If approached in position of 3, the fifth (of VII7 altered) has to be omitted.

Ex. 147

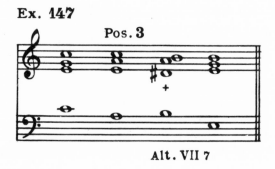

Alt. VII 7

When preceded by other degrees, as by the tonic (a), or supertonic (b), the VII7 should appear first in its diatonic form, then altered.

Ex. 148

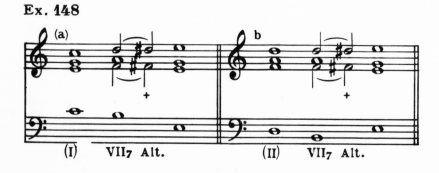

VII, altered into a V7 chord complete with chromatic and diatonic embellishments:

Ex. 149

VII 7   Alt.VII 7

EXERCISES: (The instructions provided in Chapter 16 on the use of diatonic nonharmonic tones apply generally in chromatic embellishments.)

Alter I into a V7, resolve, and continue to tonic cadence

                              in F major

                              in A major, pos. 3

Prepare, then alter II into a V7, and proceed as above

                              in G major

                              in B flat major, pos. 5

Prepare, then alter III into a V7, and continue as above

                              in B major

                              in E flat major, pos. 3

Prepare, then alter VI into a V7, and continue as above

                              in D major

                              in F major, pos. 5

Prepare, then alter VII, into a V7, and continue as above

                              in E major

                              in A flat major, pos. 5

Triads Altered Into V9 Chords

Like triads altered into V7 chords, all degrees of the scale can be converted into dominant ninth chords and resolved DIATONICALLY, except IV.

Below are dominant ninths and their diatonic resolutions:

Ex. 150

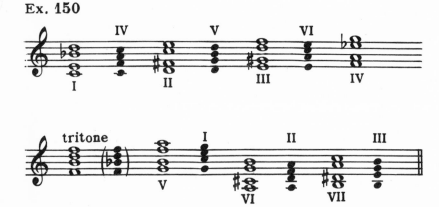

The ninth, like the seventh, commonly resolves down one degree.

Either the major or minor ninth may be employed. Otherwise, chords altered into V9 chords function in the same manner as altered V7 chords, the fifth usually being omitted in four-part writing.

Ex. 151   (I altered into a V9 chord)

(Alt.) I₉

Ex. 152 (II altered into a V9)

The altered II9 is best preceded by VI or IV.

Ex. 153 (III altered into a V9)

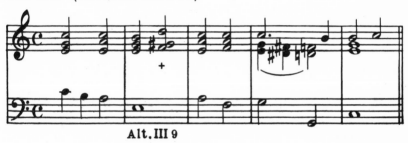

The altered III9 is best preceded by I or VI.
(The IV9 and diatonic V9 are again omitted)

Ex. 154 (VI altered into V9)

The altered VI may be preceded by either I, III or V.

Ex. 155 (VII altered into a maj. V9) To convert VII into a V9 chord, both the third and fifth are chromatically raised, in the same manner as the VII altered to V7.

VI   Alt. VII₉

The altered VII9 is best preceded by VI.

EXERCISES:

Alter I into a V9, resolve, and continue to tonic cadence
In F major

Prepare, then alter II into a V9, and continue as above
In G major

Prepare, then alter III into a V9, and continue as above
In E flat major, pos. 3

Prepare, then alter VI into a V9, and continue as above
In A major, pos. 5

Prepare, then alter VII into a V9, and continue as above
In B flat major

27. Sequence Patterns of V7 and V9 Chords

No SINGLE DEVICE was more highly favored by composers in the mid-19th century than sequence patterns of DOMINANTS. TSCHAIKOWSKY, LISZT, WAGNER, MAHLER and others utilized these sequences in countless variations. In the early part of the 20th century, forward-looking composers bitterly assailed the monotony of these devices. Nevertheless, it must be conceded that sequences of all descriptions—including altered dominants and other altered chords—frequently triggered the dramatic implications toward climaxes, especially in larger musical structures.

Granted, the abuse of sequential devices often betrays the lack of creative imagination. When artistically used, however, sequences remain one of the most powerful generators of tension.

Varied Chromatic Sequence Patterns

Alternating dominant sevenths and triads with an upward moving diatonic bass.

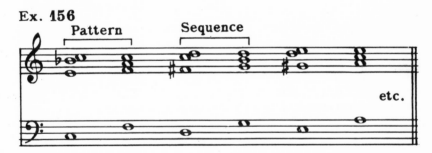

Successions of dominant seventh chords on a downward moving diatonic bass:

96

Alternating dominant seventh chords and triads on an upward moving chromatic bass:

Ex. 158

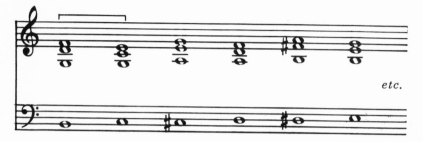

etc.

Alternating dominant major ninth chords and triads on an upward moving diatonic bass:

Ex. 159

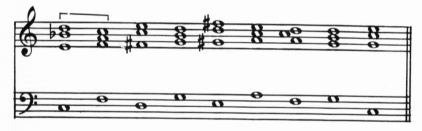

Dominant minor ninth chords alternating with dominant sevenths on a downward moving diatonic bass:

Ex. 160

Dominant minor ninth chords alternating with dominant sevenths on a downward moving chromatic bass:

Ex. 161

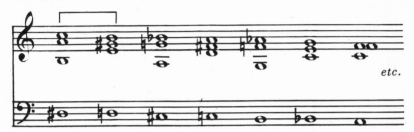

Alternating dominant minor ninth chords and triads on an upward moving chromatic bass:

Ex. 162

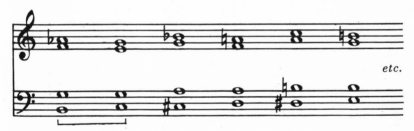

Chords altered into dominant ninths, the latter resolving on their own fundamentals. The ninth first resolves down one degree (like a suspension) on its own root before a change of harmony takes place. A, the ninth, resolves to G, the root of the chord.

Ex. 162

The following sequence illustrates this principle with dominant minor ninths and dominant major ninths alternating and resolving on their own fundamentals:

Ex. 163

7th
absent

Notice that the seventh (not the fifth) is absent in each alternate chord, with the major ninth taking its place. This procedure is in accord with rules of harmony which permit the major or minor ninth to replace the absent minor seventh.

The foregoing illustrates but a few of the endless variety of harmonic sequences which can be constructed by means of chords altered into dominants.

28. Sequences in Parallel Dominants

THE SUCCESSIONS of "synthetic" dominants have played an important role in nineteenth century music. Therefore, it is worth noting that there are instances where strictly harmonic interpretations do not hold.

For example, in the case of chords running in parallel motion scale-wise:

Ex. 164

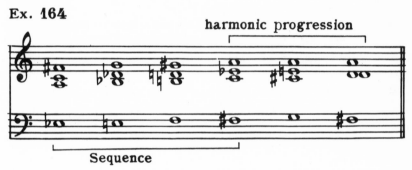

These sequences should be considered functional harmonic progressions only when the consecutive motion is disrupted in one or more of the four voices. In that case the chord immediately preceding the termination of the sequence—and the chords from there onward—should again be regarded as normal harmonic progressions.

So long as the sequence continues uninterrupted, its condition remains *status quo.** If one thinks of each chord as a new start, no concept of faulty progression is involved. This principle applies in the following sequence containing parallel fifths in the lower staff; a commonly seen succession of chromatic dominant ninths in five voices:

Ex. 165

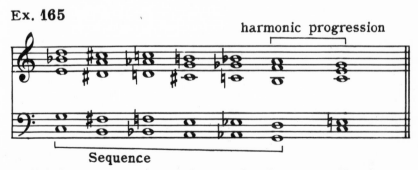

---

* "A body at rest *or in motion, if left to itself,* will maintain itself in the same condition unchanged." (Italics mine) Sir Isaac Newton, in the first of *The Three Laws of Motion.*

29. Augmented Sixth Chords

THERE STILL remain the three common species of augmented sixth chords and the Neapolitan sixth, generally built on the supertonic (II) degree.

Each species of augmented sixth chord has its own peculiar sound quality. These differences are so pronounced that they were formerly known as national in character and qualified as FRENCH, ITALIAN, and GERMAN sixth. Since they have long ago become universal in usage, their definitions no longer have special significance. Nevertheless, the student learns more quickly and retains the knowledge more securely by identifying these chords by their former national characteristics.

All augmented sixth chords should be interpreted theoretically as II chords which have been first altered into dominant seventh chords, but with this added alteration: the perfect fifth is lowered to a diminished fifth. Thus, in C major, the chord formed on D consists of the root, major third, diminished fifth and minor seventh.

Ex. 166

In each of the three forms the diminished fifth is placed in the bass, or lowest voice.

Ex. 167

Hence, the original third produces the interval of an augmented sixth from which the chord derives its name. Theoretically, however, it remains the second inversion of the altered II7b.

1) *The French Sixth* (abbreviated Fr. 6)

The French sixth contains the complete chord: root, raised third, lowered fifth and the minor seventh. With the lowered fifth in the bass, the chord appears as follows:

Ex. 168

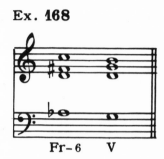

Fr-6   V

The French sixth—like all augmented sixth chords—commonly resolves into the original dominant, (V).

It is interesting to note that when the French sixth is broken into a scale, it contains four tones of the Whole-tone scale, (shown in whole notes).

Ex. 169

Thus, perhaps, it was no accident that French composers were first to make methodical use of the entire whole-tone scale, so characteristic of impressionistic music.

EXERCISES:

I—Fr. 6—V7—I in D major
           in C minor
I—VI—Fr. 6—V7—I in A flat major
              in B major, pos. 3
I—IVa—Fr. 6—Ib—V7—I in G major
               in B flat major, pos. 5

2) *The German Sixth* (abbreviated Ger. 6)

In this species the fundamental is absent, but the minor ninth is added.

Ex. 170

The German sixth in its complete form consists of the raised third, lowered fifth, minor seventh and minor ninth. With the fifth in the bass, the chord and its resolution appears as follows:

Ex. 171

Attention is called to the parallel fifths in the resolution of the German IIb to V. This is the only instance in harmonic usage where parallel fifths are permitted. HAYDN and MOZART showed a preference for the original form, with its consecutive fifths.

Ex. 172

On the other hand, BEETHOVEN, oddly enough, often deliberately avoided the parallel fifths by leading into the cadential close.

Ex. 173

Ger-6   Ib   V   I

EXERCISES:

I–Ger. 6–V–I in A flat major
              in B minor pos. 3
I–VI–Ger. 6–Ib–V7–I in A major
                     in F major pos. 3

3) *The Italian Sixth* (abbreviated It. 6)

In the Italian sixth the fundamental is absent, leaving only three tones: the raised third, lowered fifth and the minor seventh.

Ex. 174

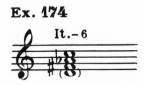

In four-part writing the original seventh is doubled, which causes this unusual situation:

Ex. 175

It.-6   V

While the seventh resolves down a semitone, as is customary, the other seventh *rises* one step, in contrary motion.

The Italian sixth, already familiar in the early 17th century, has long been favored, especially in vocal recitative passages.

Ex. 176

Monteverdi (Orfeo)

It – 6

EXERCISES:

I–It. 6–V–I in B major
              in G minor

I–VI–It. 6–V–I in E flat major
                 in D major pos. 5

30. The Neapolitan Sixth Chord

THE TRIAD on lowered IIa, known as the Neapolitan sixth (abbreviated Neap. 6), does not contain an augmented sixth. Nevertheless, it belongs in the family of altered II chords. In this form, in both major and minor, the fundamental and fifth are lowered a half-step.

Ex. 177

Like the diminished II in minor, it is used almost exclusively in the first inversion, with the bass, the original third, doubled.

Ex. 178

I   Neap-6 V

Note: In the progression Neap. IIa to V, the cross-relation between the soprano and tenor is acceptable in authentic harmony. However, it may be avoided by leading into the cadential close.

Ex. 179

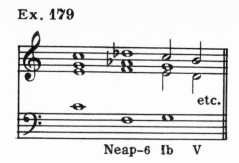

Neap-6 Ib V

The Neapolitan IIa has frequently been used as a suspension for dramatic effect in compositions, with the tonic root sustained as a pedal point in the bass.

Ex. 180

Neap – 6

I

EXERCISES:

I—Neap. 6 (IIa)—V—I in B major
in F major, pos. 3
I—Neap. 6 (IIa)—Ib—V7—I in G major
in F minor

31. Chromatic Modulation

THE FALLACY of relying on "synthetic" dominants for making modulations has been previously demonstrated. Consequently artificially calculated modulations—chromatic or any other kind—seldom work out artistically in practice. Nor is it of much help—though undoubtedly interesting— to make a study of them as used by other composers. For, if chosen as models, they would also have to duplicate or at least imitate the line of composition.

Modulation as practiced in compositions involves elements of time-spacing, melodic and rhythmic tensions and structural considerations that are never the same. Therefore, only two procedures can be described, either of which must be applied in a composition. To illustrate this we show two examples of a chromatic modulation from C to C sharp major, utilizing these two methods of approach.

First method: By means of *rhythmic* and *melodic* artifice used to presage a radical harmonic turn.

Ex. 181

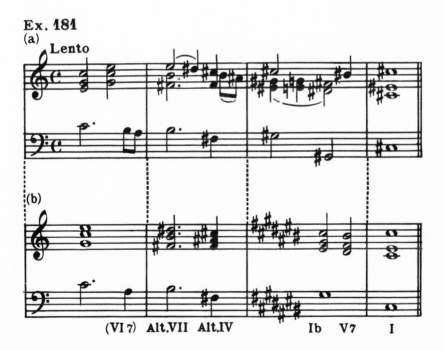

(VI 7)   Alt.VII   Alt.IV   Ib   V7   I

Two basic progressions are used here to prepare this distant modulation: 1) The C, in the bass (at bar one) arrives on the note A via the passing tone. This in turn produces the illusion of a Neap. 6, in the C-triad above it. 2) The suspension of the E in the soprano (bar two) delays the D sharp resolution into the third quarter. Thus, the resolution into the B major triad, accomplished by *time-spacing*, brings the modulation to a smooth cadence, almost diatonic in its effect. Example 181b shows the harmonic outline of the modulation.

Second Method: By means of *sequence patterns* of chromatically altered chords.

Ex. 182

The above modulation consists of three *upward* moving chromatic sequence patterns which carry the modulation first from C to D, then to E major. The third pattern brings the modulation directly to the cadence in the new key, C sharp major.

Another example of modulation by sequence, A major to C minor, shows the same method employed on a *downward* moving sequence pattern.

The latter method, though much misused, is still effective. It must be emphasized that none of these modulations—even though smoothly contrived—have the *musical* substance to bring it to life. Modulations are almost wholly dependent on compositional factors and are never alike. Consequently, they cannot be theoretically planned. Nonetheless, the student can profit from a thorough knowledge of these two types of chromatic modulation.

EXERCISES:

Make various chromatic modulations to distant keys incorporating the first method.

Make various chromatic modulations to distant keys, using the second method.

Ex. 183

Resume of Part Two

IT WAS disclosed that chromatic, like diatonic processes, can be narrowed down to a limited number of altered chords. These are: chromatically altered TRIADS; chords altered into DOMINANTS; the three species of augmented sixth chords—the ITALIAN, GERMAN, and FRENCH SIXTH; and the NEAPOLITAN SIXTH. It was also pointed out that the general practice of teaching modulations by means of altered dominant sevenths, ninths, etc.—or dominants of any kind—is misleading. This procedure may at best be termed *modulatory progression*, rather than modulation, proper.

Finally, it was demonstrated that genuine CHROMATIC MODULATION can be achieved by only two methods, to which *all* chromatic modulations must adhere. In other words, chromatic modulation, except as abstract exercises, cannot in fact be taught.

Thus, the paradox remains that DIATONIC MODULATION, though rarely encountered in compositions, is the only absolute form of modulation. All other kinds are arbitrary.

"The ENHARMONIC changes in their widest range are the
natural adversaries of a good melody, but their effect is
mysterious and surprising. They represent the wide
world, which dissolves the familiar, produces many il-
lusions and clothes the unsubstantial with a certain
splendor, leaving it difficult to decide which is reality
and which is deception."*

PART THREE

ENHARMONIC PROCESSES

32. Enharmonic Processes

Enharmonic Music

THE TERMS DIATONIC and CHROMATIC are used freely by musicians, but
the mere mention of the expression ENHARMONIC MUSIC will generally
draw a blank stare. Yet, if music largely consisting of diatonic tones
is named diatonic music, and that which incorporates the use of chromatic intervals and chords chromatic music, then logically, music employing the liberal use of enharmonic changes should be called *enharmonic music*.

In practice, at least, we know a great deal about chords of the diatonic and chromatic scales. On this subject the classical and romantic
composers left little to be added by their successors. On the other
hand, the significance of enharmonic factors is as puzzling and mysterious today as ever. Precise investigation is lacking. Compared to diatonic and chromatic processes the few enharmonic changes and their
equivalents treated in traditional harmony are so limited as to remain
an unknown quantity. (See Chapter 42)

---

* Simon Sechter, *Die Richtige Folge der Grundharmonien.* (Translated by C. C.
Muller 1871.)

The study of enharmonic changes taken up in harmony comprises the exposition of only three chords, specifically: the AUGMENTED TRIAD, the DIMINISHED SEVENTH and the DOMINANT SEVENTH.

Enharmonic Change

An enharmonic change occurs when two tones, although having the same sound, are written (or spelled) differently. For example: C sharp, when written D flat, constitutes an enharmonic change.*

---

* Before the tempered scale (equal temperament) came into use, there was a difference in pitch in the enharmonic change from a sharp to a flat and vice-versa. However, harmony, as we know it, is based on the tempered scale.

33. Enharmonic Changes of the Augmented Triad

WHEN ONE TONE of a chord (rarely two) is enharmonically changed, the chord is said to have changed its equivalent. This means, in turn, that the function of the whole chord has assumed a *different harmonic relationship*. Let us see how this works.

An augmented triad may be enharmonically exchanged twice.

To an augmented triad formed a major third higher;

and to an augmented triad formed a major third lower.

They are, of course, each time precisely the same tones.

Augmented triads have two common resolutions, to the major triad a perfect fifth lower and to the minor triad a third lower. In each case the lowest note of the triad assumes the function of a NEW ROOT.

Below, an augmented triad on C, resolved both ways.

Ex. 184

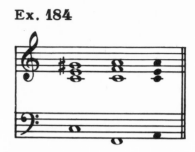

Now, exchanged enharmonically to a triad a third higher, on E, and resolved both ways.

Ex. 185

Then, exchanged enharmonically to a triad a third lower, on A flat, and resolved both ways.

Ex. 186

Thus, an augmented triad may potentially resolve into SIX DIFFERENT KEYS—three major and three minor. Below is the identical example showing each of the six possible keys of resolution with the three upper voices remaining in the same relative position.

Ex. 187

F   (a)   A   (c♯)   D♭ (f)

EXERCISES:

Form an augmented triad on B flat. Exchange enharmonically, as given above, and resolve six ways.

Form an augmented triad on E flat. Exchange enharmonically, as given above, and resolve six ways.

34. Enharmonic Changes of the Diminished Seventh Chord

A DIMINISHED seventh chord may be enharmonically changed three times:

to a diminished seventh chord formed a minor third higher;

to a diminished seventh chord formed a minor third lower;

and to a diminished seventh chord formed two minor thirds lower.

Diminished seventh chords are to be construed as the four upper tones of a minor V9 chord with the fundamental absent.

Hence the chord resolves, as all V9 chords, into a triad a perfect fourth above.

Below, a diminished seventh chord formed on B, and its resolution.

Ex. 188

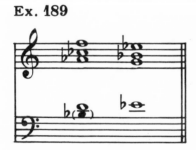

Exchanged enharmonically to a diminished seventh a minor third higher on D, with resolution in its changed equivalent.

Ex. 189

Exchanged enharmonically to a diminished seventh a minor third lower, on G sharp, with resolution in its changed equivalent.

Ex. 190

Exchanged enharmonically to a diminished seventh TWO minor thirds lower, on E sharp, with resolution in its changed equivalent.

Ex. 191

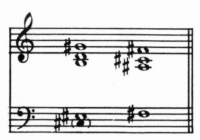

Thus, a diminished seventh chord has the potentiality of resolving into *four different major or minor keys.* Below are the identical examples showing each of the four possible keys of resolution with the upper voices remaining in the same relative position.

Ex. 192

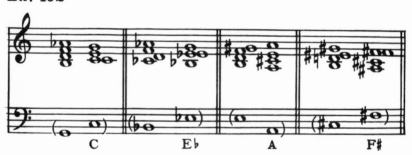

EXERCISES:

Construct a diminished seventh chord on B sharp. Exchange enharmonically, as given above, and resolve four ways.

Construct a diminished seventh chord on C sharp. Exchange enharmonically as given above, and resolve four ways. (See Chapter 42)

35. Enharmonic Change of the Dominant V7c into an Augmented Sixth

To CONVERT the dominant seventh chord into an augmented sixth chord, first change the seventh into its enharmonic equivalent of the *degree below*. In C major, for instance, F, the seventh of V7, is enharmonically changed to E sharp, thus creating the interval of an augmented sixth.

Ex. 193

In this form of enharmonic change, the third inversion, V7c, with the seventh in the bass, is most frequently used. We first show the V7c resolving, as usual, into the Ia.

Ex. 194

V7c   Ia

Then, with the bass, F, enharmonically changed to E sharp, resolving into F sharp major, its new equivalent.

Ex. 195

In this extraordinary exchange the key of C major is automatically converted into F sharp major, in one single progression. (See Ex. 223, Chapter 43.) This becomes possible because the E sharp now functions as a leading-tone which resolves up a semitone to F sharp major, the NEW TONIC. The G major triad above the E sharp, on the other hand, may be interpreted as having been transformed into a Neap. 6th CHORD, which resolves, as it commonly does, a semitone down into F sharp major, the NEW TONIC.

Ex. 196

Neap-6   I

The harmonic significance of this dualism may best be seen in the example below.

Ex. 197

The enharmonic exchange of the chord is shown in whole notes, with the rest of the implied harmony in shaded notes. When all three staves are sounded together, the startling, yet logical result is obvious.

EXERCISES:

Form a dominant V7c on F, pos. 3

Form a dominant V7c on B, pos. 8

Directions: Resolve each into Ia, change the bass into the enharmonic equivalent of the degree below and resolve in accordance with its newly gained relationship.

36. Enharmonic Modulation

THE LAST EXAMPLE cogently illustrates the feasibility of a modulation to a distant tonality in a single progression.

Thus, it may readily be seen that in enharmonic modulation, as in chromatic modulation, no clear-cut rules or exact methods of procedure are applicable.

Below we give an example of an enharmonic modulation based on each type of enharmonic change: the augmented triad (Ex. 198), the diminished seventh (Ex. 199), and the exchange of the dominant V7c into an augmented sixth (Ex. 200). The modulations are divided into three sections: a) establishment of tonality; b) modulation by enharmonic exchange; and c) cadence in the new key.

Ex. 198

Ex. 199

Ex. 200

Each of the above modulations has been accomplished by a single enharmonic change. It must be re-emphasized, however, that only experience, plus a modicum of creative application, are the final criteria for making modulations, no matter of what genre.

37. Enharmonic Changes Which are Nonharmonic

ENHARMONIC CHANGES sometimes occur in orchestral scoring for individual instruments, for reasons technical rather than harmonic. On most string instruments, for example, many flats are simpler to execute than sharps. Hence, a passage written in C sharp major, as shown below, is much easier to execute on the violin if enharmonically changed to D flat major.

Ex. 201

Franz Liszt-Sonate for Violin and Piano

Enharmonic changes for nonharmonic purposes are most frequent on the harp, due to the nature of its pedal structure.

Ex. 202

These are external differences and should not be mistaken for enhar-monic changes which are functional.

38. Synthesis of Parts I, II and III

A COMPLETE LISTING of all the basic chords in harmony follows:

PART I. DIATONIC: Thirteen basic chords.

PART II. CHROMATIC: One basic chord (the French sixth).

PART III. ENHARMONIC: None; no actual new chord emerges.

Thus, the final count (in white notes) remains FOURTEEN BASIC CHORDS and their inversions. These are:

Ex. 203   The FOUR primary triads;

The SEVEN different seventh chords of the harmonic minor scale;

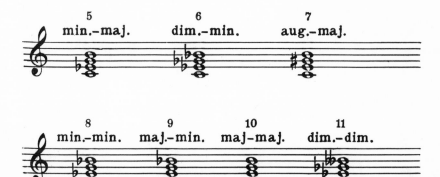

The TWO, major and minor, V9 chords,

and lastly, the FRENCH SIXTH.

On the other hand, if all chromatic and enharmonic chords repeated in different contexts are included as BASIC CHORDS, then the total number (in shaded notes) is extended to TWENTY-THREE.

These comprise the two enharmonic changes of AUGMENTED TRIADS;

the GERMAN, ITALIAN and NEAPOLITAN sixths;

the three enharmonic changes of the DIMINISHED SEVENTH CHORD,

and the enharmonic change of the V7 into an AUGMENTED SIXTH CHORD.

A Brief Outline of the Evolution of Harmony

Music, like all the other arts, derives from nature. Perhaps primitive man's first expressions of song were his utterances of pain, love and mourning. Among musicologists it is common knowledge that some of the Asian and African dialects and languages were responsible for the earliest intoned musical intervals and cadences.

The first melodic sounds observed among the primitives which can be recognized as musical structures were intervals of the second:

(Central American)   (American Indian)

From: The History of Melody, Bence Szabolcsi (Edition Cserepfalxi, B'pest.)

Then came thirds, fourths, fifths and octaves, etc.

Song from BUKA (Solomon Islands) after Sachs

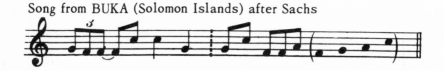

From these intervals the pentatonic (five-tone) scales emerged. They prevailed for many centuries in lands widely separated geographically. Thus, for hundreds of years—perhaps thousands—pentatonic scales were the foundations of art music as well as folk music.*

The early peoples among whom these melodies predominated were the Chinese, Negro, Hungarian, Scottish and the American Indian, to name a few. In fact, pentatonic melodies of both ancient and modern vintage are still alive in musical repertoire.

---

* "Through Kodaly's stimulation—I became acquainted with the works of Debussy. I observed with great astonishment that in his music pentatonic turns similar to those found in our folk music played a dominant role. Similar tendencies are to be observed in the music of Igor Stravinsky." (From Bela Bartok's autobiographical sketch, prepared by him in 1922.)

Transylvanian – Hungarian folk song (ca 1000 – 1200)
Lento – Rubato

Edited by Béla Bartók and Zoltan Kodaly

Until the latter part of the Middle Ages, which coincides with the early beginnings of harmony in the Western world (ca. 1000–1400), harmonies consisted mainly of two-part counterpoint using combinations of fourths, fifths and octaves.

Ex. 204
Perotinus – 1200

Only much later, between the thirteenth and fifteenth centuries, was the THIRD established as a consonance which led inevitably to TRIADS, the foundation of our harmonic system.

As harmony progressed and expanded, conspicuous changes occurred periodically. And though the shift from one harmonic style to another was gradual, these mutations crystallized in their cadence forms, where each change of style may be clearly observed. The following cadences were selected at random as being generic to their respective eras.

Renaissance Cadences

Ballata (14th century).

Although harmonies of FOURTHS and FIFTHS still predominate, triadic tendencies are clearly evident.

Ex. 205
FRANCESCO LANDINI   (14th century)

By the 15th century, accented TRIADS occur more frequently. Mark the resemblance to modern three-part choral writing.

Ex. 206
GILLES BINCHOIS   (15th century)

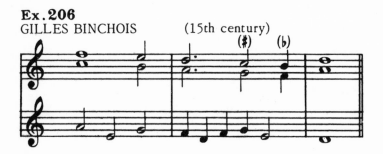

One of the earliest examples of FOUR-PART triadic writing with plagal close:

Ex. 207
BARTOLOMEO TROMBONCINO   (early 16th century)

Baroque Cadences

Note the minor tonic (*tierce de picardie*) preceding the D major cadence:

Ex.208
ORLANDO LASSUS   (Latter 16th century)

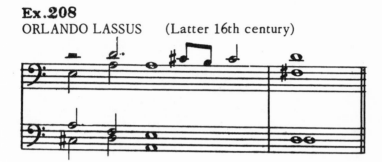

Viadana was one of the first composers, along with John Dowland and several other madrigalists, to make independent use of the DOMI-NANT SEVENTH chord:

Ex.209
LUDOVICO VIADANA   (early 17th century)

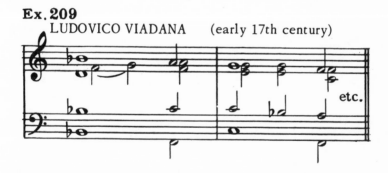

etc.

This is an early example of a CADENTIAL-LIKE close. Approached through the diminished seventh chord, it shows the major-minor mode well established:

Ex. 210
G. CARISSIMI   (mid 17th century)

134

Once firmly implanted, harmony reached its first peak around the mid-16th century. By then the merging of homophonic—that is—chordal —writing, with melody, had revolutionized harmony.

Baroque to Classical Cadences

From the mid-17th to the mid-18th century cadences were characterized by the more liberal use of ACCENTED APPOGIATURA.

Ex. 211

CLAUDEO MONTEVERDI (1642)

Harmony gained further impetus during the latter part of the 16th and early part of the 17th centuries through the expansion of the CHROMATIC SCALE. That was the great experimental period of the Italian Madrigalists headed by CARLOS GESUALDO, LUCA MORENZEO* and CLAUDEO MONTEVERDI. To their names should be added the English Madrigalists JOHN DOWLAND, WILLIAM BYRD, THOMAS WEELKES and others. It was a remarkable era of iconoclastic composers who were, in some respects, several centuries ahead of their time.

This remarkable chromatic era reached fruition in the works of BACH and HANDEL.

Rococo or Early Classical Cadences

Ex. 212

J. S. BACH Well-Tempered Clavier (1685-1750)

* (See Ex. 241 in Part IV.)

Ex. 213

G. F. HANDEL (1685-1759)   Largo

Mid-Classical Cadences

In comparison with the 16th and 17th century chromaticists, harmony during the classical period became synthesized. It was a period of adjustment when music followed more severe and conservative lines. Characterized by strict adherence to tonality, music of the mid-eighteenth to early nineteenth century was more symmetrical, and cadence forms were more or less uniform. They are marked by increasing application of plain, unadorned, chords and symmetrical rhythms, frequently repeated for dynamic purposes. On the whole, there is less use of accented appogiaturas.

Ex. 214

JOSEF HAYDN   Piano Sonata no. 2

Ex. 215

W.A. MOZART Symphony D maj. K. 504

Ex. 216
L.V. BEETHOVEN

Piano Sonata op. 7
(a)

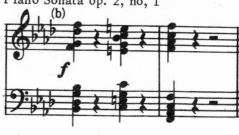

Piano Sonata op. 2, no, 1
(b)

Ex. 217
FRANZ SCHUBERT Unfinished Symphony

The exceptions are the introductions and slow movements in symphonic and chamber music, where the Bach type of free-fantasy-embellishments still prevail.

Except for an occasional accented appogiatura, suspension or anticipation, the classical masters seemed content with the ordinary IV, or II–V–I cadences. On the other hand, tension achieved by dynamic repetition of the same chord was most effectively used by them.

Note: For two examples which seem to stretch dynamic repetitions of a chord to its limit, see the end of the first movement in *Beethoven's Symphony No. 1* (the tonic triad is repeated for 21 measures), and the closing bars of the *Symphony No. 5* (29 bars of repeated tonic chords).

Moreover, melodic expansion through motivic design, implemented by changing tonalities, provided greater freedom through modulation and led to the immense growth of musical forms, from the simple ABA forms to the symphonic sonata structure. Although classical music represented in terms of harmony a sobering-up period, the symphonies and chamber music of HAYDN, MOZART, BEETHOVEN and SCHUBERT remain a living testimony of the tremendous accomplishments of the classical era.

Romantic Period Cadences

In marked contrast to the severity of classical cadences, the romantic school of composers initiated the "surprise" approach. In general, the *cadential, plagal* and the *IV—V—I* type of cadences remain, although cadences without the use of the dominant are more frequent. However, the constantly varied manner of approach to cadences makes them appear far more radical than they really are.

This cadence has no dominant:

Ex. 218

F. CHOPIN   Etude op. 25, no. 4

The tonic A is sustained as a pedal point under the B flat Neapolitan sixth chord, and the C sharp, in the melody, anticipates the A major cadence.

A more delightfully bewildering approach to the V—I than the example below would be difficult to find.

Ex. 219

Etude op. 10, no. 6   (b)

(Harmonic outline)

Written in the key of E flat minor, the Neap. 6th, F flat major—enharmonic equivalent of E major (at b)—is preceded by A major and followed by the ordinary V—I cadence, B flat to E flat minor. Then, as a post-cadence, the E flat minor finally resolves into E flat major (picardy third).

In this cadence the ostensible harmonic disorder has been planned with canny skill.

In the example below the F minor triad (submediant) is superimposed over the normal V—I cadence.

Ex. 220
R. SCHUMANN   Phantasiestücke op. 12

Later in the same composition, the plain cadential close has a star-tling effect, as it follows the thrice repeated diminished seventh chord. It shows that this chord had by no means lost its dramatic impact after Mozart and Beethoven.

Ex. 221

(Harmonic outline)

Without a doubt the most daring harmonic iconoclast of his time, FRANZ LISZT, saw far into the future.

Below is another singular example of the Neap. 6th—enharmonically changed to A major—used in a surprising cadence in A flat major.

Ex. 222
F. LISZT   Années de Pèlerinage

dolce   etc.

The calm and peaceful closing bars of the overwhelming *B Minor Sonata* avoid any illusion to a routine cadence. The only relationship that can logically justify this cadence harmonically would be through the hypo-phrygian scale. This approach to the cadence, considered madness at the time, anticipated similar methods of merging the new with the old much used later by the impressionistic composers.

Ex. 223
Piano Sonata in B minor

Below is another cadence quite different from other romantic composers.

Ex. 223 a
P. I. TCHAIKOWSKI   Romeo and Juliet

Notice the poignant effect of the dissonances in the horn (middle staff) against a routine diatonic sequence consisting of II–VI–V–I.

The romantic and post-romantic periods of the latter part of the nineteenth century became the springboard for a new age of chromatic expansion during which harmonic coloration and orchestral brilliance reached their zenith. Harmony, seemingly stretched to its limit by WAGNER, LISZT, STRAUSS and MAHLER, then went beyond to impressionism by SATIE, DEBUSSY and RAVEL.

Impressionistic Cadences

The chief trait in cadences of the impressionistic composers is the purposeful avoidance of a feeling of finality. Omission of the direct dominant-tonic cadence leaves the composition—so to speak—hanging in the air, resulting in the undefined cadence. Consonant sensation is obscured (1) by subtle use of the so-called mixed modal close:

(The cadence shown below fluctuates between C-major and A-minor.)

Ex. 224

MAURICE RAVEL   Ma mere l'oye

(2) by superimposing foreign tones or chords over the main harmony. The precedent for this device, variously called escape-tones, cluster-chords, etc. was already well established—albeit in a rough form—by RICHARD STRAUSS.

Ex. 225

RICHARD STRAUSS   Der Rosenkavalier

It was left to the impressionists, however, to take full advantage of this artifice.

Ex. 226
MAURICE RAVEL   Piano Sonatine

Here the F sharp major cadence is preceded by the lowered III (mediant). The resolution is further obscured by the added escape-tone G sharp.

This mixed modal ending consists of both the D sharp and F sharp major triad. The superimposed "escape-tone" C sharp adds a further ethereal quality to the cadence.

Ex. 227
CLAUDE DEBUSSY   Pelléas et Mélisande

We have left for the last example the ending that may well claim first rank among the best known impressionistic cadences. The unforgettable impression left is due, in this case, not so much to the mixed modal ending in the last three measures. That is typical. Rather, it is to be found in the dazzling succession of nonharmonic (escape) triads in the first bar which leads to the cadence.

Ex. 228
CLAUDE DEBUSSY   L'apres midi d'un Faune

In the works of ZOLTAN KODALY we find some unusual cadences, not of the impressionistic or the very dissonant contemporary type. They are somewhere in between.

Ex. 229
ZOLTAN KODALY   Psalmus Hungaricus

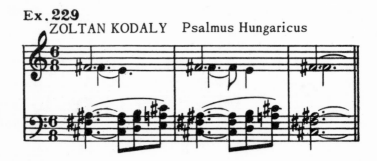

This interesting modal type cadence is left suspended on the F sharp major resolution in the *second inversion*.

Below, a Kodaly-type of cluster chord—consisting of a telescoped double-triad—leaving the cadence suspended in mid-air.

Ex. 230

On the threshold of the twentieth century it was inevitable that harmony should lead directly to the dissonant techniques of our time.

Twentieth Century Cadences

Abruptness is the chief characteristic of contemporary cadences. Frequently the endings are so sudden as to give the impression of being severed. The apparent lack of a fixed tonality is typical, the harmonic factor being secondary, at least as regards previously understood relationships. Hence, abrupt endings and absence of defined tonality, are the main peculiarities of 20th century cadences.

The example below, an early and elementary specimen of the abrupt ending, aptly sets the *modus operandi* of the 20th century cadence.

Ex. 231
IGOR STRAVINSKY   Petroushka

Although diatonic to the key of F major, note the absence of the customary IV—V—I connotation in the harmonic sense. The repeated F's in the last bar serve as a "codetta."

In the next example, the basic harmony (seen in the upper staff) consists of the C major triad with an F sharp added. The melodic line (in the middle staff) runs in parallel fourths. And the upward moving whole-tone scale further upsets the tonal stability. It hardly need be pointed out that this cadence represents the acme of abruptness.

Ex 232

IGOR STRAVINSKY   The Rite of Spring

Cadences in slower movements are no less abrupt than in the faster movements, as may be seen by the two ensuing examples.

Ex. 233

ANTON WEBERN   Variations for Piano

Ex. 234 *

ARNOLD SCHOENBERG   Ode to Napoleon op. 41

The chamber works of BELA BARTOK, particularly his six string quartets, represent some of his greatest achievements. The cadences in these works, especially the final ones, have more than ordinary significance.

The *Third String Quartet* (at a) ends in C sharp, with the fifths D sharp and A sharp superimposed.

Ex. 235

BELA BARTOK   3rd String Quartet

---

* In Example 234 we call attention to the similarity, purely co-incidental, to the whole-tone scale cadence No. 11, Chapter 42.

The *Fourth String Quartet* (b) ends on a C major-minor triad.*

4th String Quartet

The *Fifth Quartet* (c) terminates on the unison, B flat; and *Music for Strings, Percussion and Celeste* terminates on a downward sequence of four triads starting with the tritone on D sharp, then C sharp minor, B major, and ending on the final tonic, A major.

5th String Quartet

Music For Strings, Percussion and Celeste

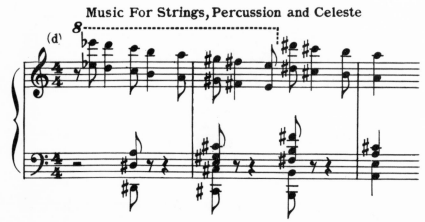

* See Example 255 and 256.

PART FOUR

HARMONY PROBLEMS
OLD AND NEW

39. The Quandary of the Chromatic Scale
and the Tritone

EXAMPLES 236a and b show the ascending and descending chromatic scales in four-part harmonization. Each chromatically raised or lowered tone has been converted into a V7 chord, upward, or V9 chord downward (in shaded notes), which resolve into their diatonic constituents.

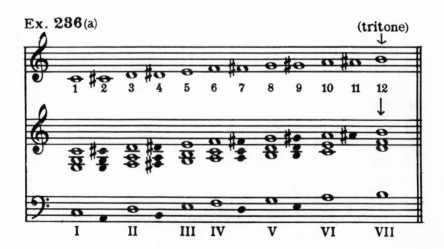

Ex. 236(a)

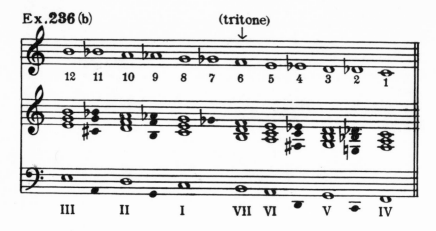

Notice that the raised VI, A sharp, in ascending (a) and the lowered V, G flat, in descending (b) both resolve into the same *tritone*.

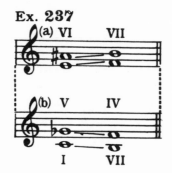

If the tritone is to be avoided, the only alternative must resolve out of key.

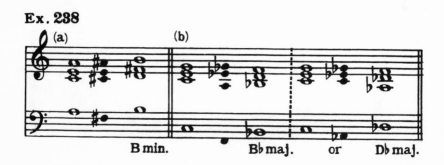

To avoid the tritone conflict and yet preserve the diatonic relationship, we lower VII-B to B flat on the ascending chromatic scale (a) and raise IV-F to F sharp on the descending scale (b), thus enabling both to resolve into diatonic consonances.

Ex. 239

The above demonstration indicates that the tritone does not permit all twelve tones of the chromatic scale to function with absolute harmonic equality. The tritone, let us call it *the tone of modulation,* must be left open—held in reserve—for the sake of variety. Accordingly, ELEVEN TONES at most—not TWELVE—have equal harmonic status.

40. The Diminished Seventh, Chord of the Double Tritone

THE DIMINISHED seventh chord is defined in harmony textbooks simply as a dominant minor V9 chord minus the root. No reference is made to its past significance. Yet, although generally viewed today with disdain by the sophisticated musician, the diminished seventh chord stands out—in the light of the history of harmonic development—as the most powerful, versatile and intricate among the FOURTEEN BASIC CHORDS in harmony.

The enharmonic equivalents of the diminished seventh chord (1)—formed here on E sharp—and their resolutions (2), plus the implied fundamentals (3) when combined, add up to the twelve tones of the chromatic scale. (1, 2 and 3 in shaded notes)

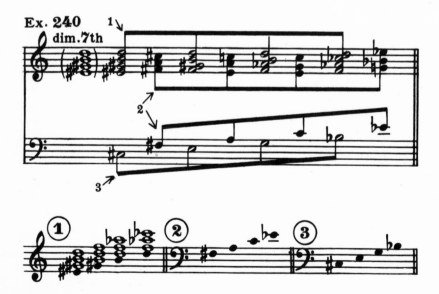

The extraordinary chromatic and enharmonic implications of this chord—especially as revealed in its thorough exploitation by the classical and romantic composers—made it the chord of a thousand hues. Frequently used as the crucial chord in reaching the climax in a composition, no other chord emphasizes more dramatically the potential contained in a single basic chord. (See Secondary Seventh Chords.)

We list a few of the many striking examples in which the diminished seventh chord leads up to—or is itself—the climax chord.

MOZART: *Symphony in G minor* (K-550): 1st movement, bars 153–160
Finale, bars 188–205
MOZART: *String quartet* (K-465): 1st movement, bars 121–145
MOZART: *String quintet* (K-516): 3rd movement, bars 18–22
BEETHOVEN: *Symphony No. 5:* 1st movement, bars 160–180
also bars 269–300
CHOPIN: *Prelude No. 19:* Bars 22–32
LISZT: *Piano Sonata in B-minor:* At beginning of coda
(Allegro Moderato)
LISZT: *Les Preludes:* Bars 155–160

41. Thirds, Tritones and Chromatics

Odd Chromatic Passages From Gesualdo to Bartok

IN THE EXAMPLES shown below, written some three centuries apart, the similarity of harmonic devices, in the use of rising thirds in the bass against descending chromatics, is extraordinary. The more so, since it is inconceivable that either LISZT or WAGNER ever heard of MORENZEO or GESUALDO. Research into the chromatic exploits of these almost forgotten geniuses had not yet been undertaken at that time. It is not unlikely, however, that WAGNER may have been familiar with the passage in LISZT's *Faust Symphony,* which preceded *Valkyre* by more than a decade.*

Ex. 241

LUCA MORENZEO 'Solo Pensoso' (1550-1599)

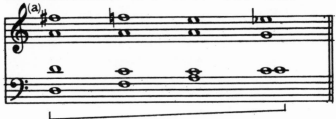

CARLO GESUALDO 'Moro Lasso' (1560-1611)

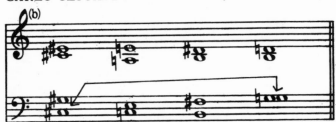

* "It is quite possible that the earlier Wagner owed much to Franz Liszt. It is my impression that the influence of Liszt on the music of the future is stronger than that of Richard Wagner." From Bela Bartok's lecture on Franz Liszt Problems, given at the Budapest Academy of Science, in 1936.

"They are part of the splendid adventure which, at a given stage, brought Wagner into touch with . . . Liszt, whom he (Wagner) conscientiously plagiarized and who met him with nothing but a kindly smile of acquiescence." (*Monsieur Croche* by Claude Debussy; translated by Lawrence Gilman, published by The Viking Press, N.Y.)

RICHARD WAGNER   'Walkure' (1869)

FRANZ LISZT   'Faust Symphony' (1856)

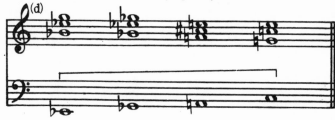

At a, the bass consists of alternating minor and major thirds.

At b, note the tendency of the *tritone* to take shape in the bass.

At c, the bass rises two minor thirds (tritone), then a semitone.

At d, the diminished seventh chord in the bass—the double tritone—is complete.

The next two examples have similar patterns of thirds and tritones in the bass, but the upper parts are very different.

Here the bass pattern consists of descending dominant seventh intervals followed by a diminished seventh, and the upper voice contains the intervals of the descending harmonic (F) minor scale.

Ex. 242
BEETHOVEN   Piano Sonata op. 13

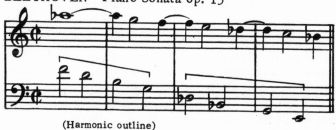

(Harmonic outline)

Example 243 has an ascending pattern of *major triads* formed over the intervals of the *diminished seventh* chord.

Ex. 243
RAVEL   String Quartet

A unique tonal passage occurs in the final movement of BARTOK's Third Piano Concerto, his last work.

Ex. 244
BARTOK   3rd Piano Concerto (bars 183-197)

(Harmonic outline)

This orchestral passage which underlines the solo piano (the solo part is not included in the sketch) flits by almost unnoticed. Yet the effect may be likened to that of a balloon as it collapses. The passage seems gradually to evaporate. Observe that in the upper staff the first seven tones (E sharp to F sharp) correspond to the scale of *F sharp major*, and the next seven tones parallel the scale of *C major*. Thus the passage modulates from F sharp to C major, in the shape of a DOUBLE DIATONIC SCALE encompassing the entire chromatic scale. Nevertheless, it sounds as smooth as a diatonic modulation.*

* There is a parallel—in reverse—between this passage and the enharmonic change of the V7c (in C major) into an augmented sixth resolving into F# major. (Refer to Chapter 35.)

42. The Whole-Tone Scale as a Seven-Part Chord

THE CHROMATIC scale can be divided into two sets of whole-tone scales, each a half-step apart.

Ex. 245

I   II   III   IV   V   V

I   II   III   IV   V   VI

The whole-tone scale contains no consonant triads and cannot, therefore, suggest a tonality. If arranged, however, into a six-tone chord, with a seventh voice added in the bass to represent the *dominant degree,* then a logical and correct resolution may be effected into the *tonic* of any of the twenty-four major and minor keys.

In order that each key change may be unmistakably recognized, the six-tone (doubly augmented) chord is retained throughout in the same relative position. The spelling of the following seven-voice chords has been adjusted to conform as closely as possible with the rules of correct harmonic resolution.

Supp. VII–2

Observe that one tone, the tone which represents the *dominant* is doubled in bars 2, 4, 6, 8, 10 and 12.

Ex. 246

First Set   Major Resolution

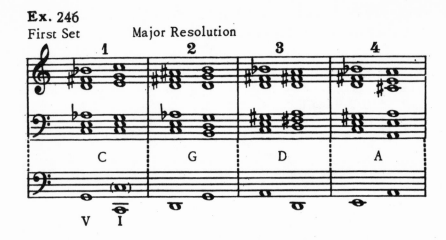

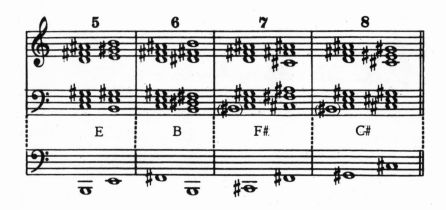

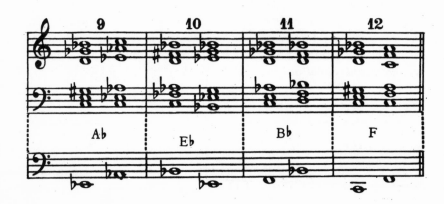

Supp. VII–3

Second Set: Bars 1, 3, 5, 7, 9 and 11 double the dominant tone.

Ex. 247
Second Set   Minor Resolution

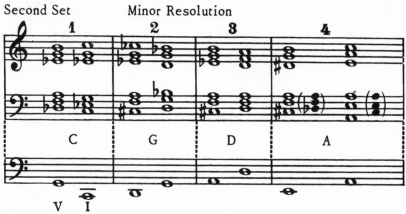

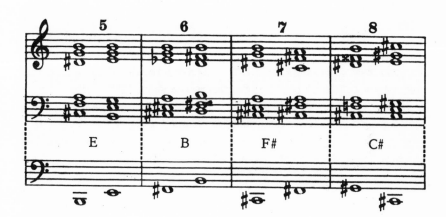

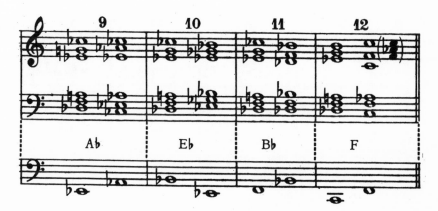

Supp. VII–4

Note: Although the twelve cadences in the first set resolve into *major* and those of the second set into *minor*, they are equally effective when reversed.

43. An Experiment in the Church Modes and the C Major Scale

THE CHURCH—or ecclesiastical modes—were the prevailing musical system for many centuries before they were gradually replaced by the major-minor system (harmony) between the years 1300–1600.

In the church modes, the first tone of each represented a center tone called *finalis*, which was comparable to our tonic (at a). Taking the first note of each church mode and transposing it to start each time on the note C, results in the transpositions shown at b.

Ex. 248

When the keys implied in each transposed mode are properly placed together (at c) they form the scale of A flat major.

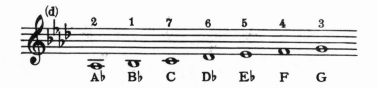

If we then take the starting notes of the original church modes, beginning with the note C—synonymous with the C major scale—and play the A flat major scale (also starting on the note C) in contrary motion, they spell out the so-called MIRROR or CRAB scale.*

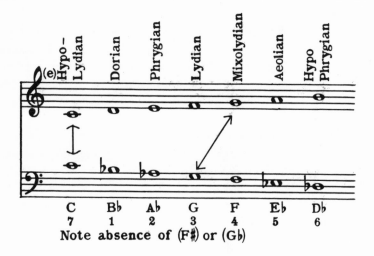

Note absence of (F♯) or (G♭)

Notice that both scales contain the intervals of the tonic and dominant degrees C and G. Furthermore, the tones of both scales combined, make up the chromatic scale minus one tone, the F sharp (or G flat), the interval of the TRITONE. (See Example 239.)

The above experiment seems to bear out the theory that this change from an older to a newer system was more evolutionary than revolutionary.

---

* During the mid-Middle Ages the use of the C major scale, in its newly discovered harmonic context, was called Modus Lascivus (the "wanton mode") and was forbidden.

44. An Experiment in Minor Scales and Modes

Hypothetical Church Modes Formed on the Harmonic Minor Scale

EMPLOYING THE same procedure as in the previous example, an experiment follows: Instead of the notes of the C-major scale, we will use only the notes involved in the harmonic minor scale on A, the relative minor of C-major, thus fashioning a hypothetical set of church modes in harmonic minor.

Since the C-major framework of the *Dorian mode* begins on D, the second degree, we will construct a hypothetical *Dorian mode* starting on B (the second degree of the harmonic A minor scale) and continue with the *Phrygian mode* on C (the third degree) etc. (Ex. 249a). Observe that the G sharp is retained in each one of the hypothetical modes.

As in the previous experiment, we transpose the minor modes to commence on the same tone, this time, obviously on the note A (at b). Example 249c shows the seven implied harmonic minor keys.

Ex. 249

Hypothetical Church Mode

When the seven harmonic minor keys inherent in each transposed mode (at c) are placed together in order, they form the scale shown at d.

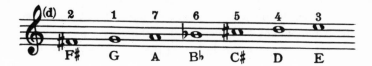

Finally, we invert scale No. 7—the original A minor—to form as before, the CRAB or MIRROR scale (at e).

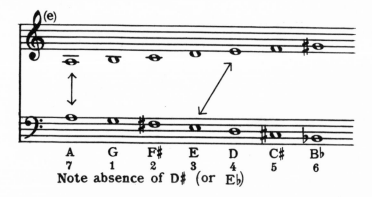

Here both scales contain the tonic and dominant degrees A and E. The missing TRITONE from the combined scales now is D sharp (or E flat).

Although the tones remain identical, each one has been converted into a different scale or mode. Moreover, notice that scale No. 4 (Ex. 249a) has a *major triad* on the first degree, and might, therefore, be construed as a major scale. Scale No. 5, on the other hand, contains both the *major* and the *minor triads* (at a, G sharp = A flat; at b, B sharp = C natural) on the first degree. To the seven different minor scales which form this hypothetical set of church modes let us include the so-called MELODIC MINOR ascending and descending scales. This makes a total of NINE minor (or minor-like) scales. Furthermore, another glance at the Dorian, Phrygian and Aeolian modes of the *Authentic* church modes (Ex. 248a) reveals these scales also to be a form of *minor*. Many other scales, such as the Hungarian, Oriental etc. also have this minor quality.

The above experiment proves the extreme ambiguity of all minor scales and/or modes. The question, therefore, is: how minor should a scale be in order to be judged a *minor mode?* What characteristics determine a minor scale? Is there such a thing as a *minor scale?* On the basis of these tests we conclude that the true function of the minor modes and their many diverse facets have never been fully investigated, least of all integrated into our harmonic perimeter.

45. Thoughts and Conjectures

IN THE PAST half century we have witnessed the emergence of systems and formulae for the partial replacement—and in some instances, the total negation—of harmony. The disturbing fact remains that no comprehensive understanding has been reached to clarify these techniques for even those musicians most sympathetic to them.

One cannot, for example, harmonically analyze BARTOK's *Miraculous Mandarin* or his *Sonata for Two Pianos and Percussion*, by mere references to polytonal harmonies, polyrhythms, unresolved nonharmonic tones, etc. Nor can STRAVINSKY's *Sacre du Printemps* or his *Symphony of Psalms* be explained in terms of serial techniques. Thus, the question remains: is harmony at an end, or have we failed to notice that it has developed naturally?

We do know that traditional harmony was based on chord structures of superimposed major and minor thirds, commencing with triads. As harmony progressed from its diatonic beginnings through the chromatic and enharmonic stages (and then beyond), why wasn't more serious consideration given to the concept that our theoretic calculations might have, at some point, gone awry? And that these miscalculations (specifically excluding the validity of secondary NINTHS, ELEVENTH and THIRTEENTH chords and all their possible inversions) obstructed harmony's systematic development from following through to its logical and natural conclusion. This is by no means a new hypothesis; periodic investigations along these lines have been conducted before. Previous attempts in this direction led to a dead end; but this does not necessarily prove the incorrectness of the original premise. Whatever the case, until now ninth, eleventh and thirteenth chords have been viewed solely as individual phenomena.

Let us examine how some of these past experiments bear out our viewpoint on *chordal expansion*. For example, the intervals of SCRIABINE's so-called "mystic chord" on which this composition is allegedly based (a), when properly placed together, form the secondary thirteenth chord shown at (b).

Ex. 250

ALEXANDER SCRIABIN   Poeme opus 69 (1872-1915)

No. 53 ML

Another instance: It has been said that the persistent hammering of the passage below (a), was the original inspiration for this monumental work—which once shook the foundations of the music world.* Harmonically analyzed, it breaks down into the combination of these two common chords (at b): a V7 chord on E flat (upper staff) and an F flat major triad (lower staff).

Ex. 251

IGOR STRAVINSKY   Sacre du Printemps

No. 68 ML

Considered from the aspect of *chordal expansion*—when both chords are placed together as a seven-tone chord (seen transposed up a semitone) they form the secondary thirteenth chord shown at (c).

* See Stravinsky, *Roman Vlad* (Chapter IV), Oxford University Press, 1960.

To continue, the harmony (basic chord structure) in *Ronde Prin-taniers,* (a) from the same composition, comprises the thirteenth chord at (b).

Ex. 252

No.77 ML

Incidentally, it also spells out the scale of *D flat major.*

Chords can be broken into scales (melody) and scales can be formed into chords (harmony). Thus the eight-tone scale used by STRAVINSKY (at a)—(OLIVER MESSIEN calls it the "second mode of transposition") adds up to the secondary thirteenth chord (at b) minus the A natural.*

Ex. 253

No.79 ML

FERRUCCIO BUSONI, an indomitable explorer of new chords and harmonies, experimented with various kinds of seven-tone scales. The one shown below (at a), forms the secondary thirteenth chord (at b).

Ex. 254
BUSONI

No.78 ML

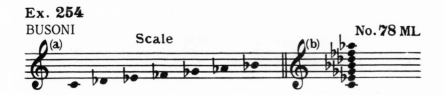

Scale

* The same eight-tone scale, formed by alternating major and minor seconds was used by Rimsky-Korsakov. (*Nicolas Slonimsky, in Thesaurus of Melodic Scales and Patterns.*)

168

Major becomes minor and vice-versa.

In *Modus Lascivus*,* in which the author shows how harmony may be extended to eighty-two basic chords, the secondary *Major-ninth* chord below implies a *Minor triad* by omitting the third and seventh in the chord;

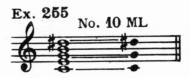

and the *minor-eleventh* chord below is converted into a *major triad* by omitting the third, seventh and ninth.

Thus, in *Modus Lascivus,* minor may become major, and major may turn into minor. Moreover, by omitting the seventh in Example 255 and the seventh and ninth in Example 256, both the C-major and C-minor triads may be simultaneously sounded; making both a part of one and the same chord (Example 257a and b). Enharmonic equivalents, too, now assume hitherto unforeseen significance.

---

* Commenced in 1944.

The predominant chord in 20th century music undoubtedly has been the DIATONIC THIRTEENTH CHORD, which is—when broken up—none other than the *C-major scale* itself.**

Ex. 258

No.47 ML

There is only room to mention a few of the many examples where this chord alone is used for many measures, both as melodic and harmonic foundation, never, it must be stressed, in the ordinary sense of dominant and tonic relationship. MAURICE RAVEL, *Rigaudon* (from *Le Tombeau de Couperin*); also in *Pavanne* (from *Ma Mere L'oye*) by the same composer. VAUGHAN WILLIAMS, *Pastoral Symphony*, IGOR STRAVINSKY's *Concerto For Piano, Orpheus*, and other of his works, and DARIUS MILHAUD's *Quartet No. 1*. To these must be added legions of European and American composers too numerous to name. Finally, BELA BARTOK, whose works abound in compositions based on the DIATONIC THIRTEENTH CHORD. At least a score of passages may be found in his *Mikrokosmos* piano cycle alone. Other examples of *chordal expansions* along similar lines could be cited ad infinitum.

It is enough to say that many 20th century composers have shown a strong leaning toward the use of some form of chordal expansion—by instinct or design—both in harmonic construction and melodic content. Significantly, and more important, all the composers mentioned used these chords in their own individual styles, thus attesting to the infinite possibilities in each *basic* chord.

If FOURTEEN BASIC CHORDS were adequate in determining three centuries of harmonic development—as demonstrated in the preceding chapters—what further potentials might be reached by the extension of harmony to a possible limit of EIGHTY-TWO BASIC CHORDS!

In our search for new sounds, may we not be losing sight of the natural continuity of harmony?

We have highlighted some old and new, strange and enigmatic manifestations in harmony, enough to indicate that one should not tamper lightly with confirmed art structures. The task of the true artist is to

** The numbered chords (at right) marked ML 10, 37, 47, 53, 68, 77, 78 and 79, are listed according to their arranged order, in the author's *Modus Lascivus*.

express his originality while being ever mindful of the rules which bind him to his art. The first objective, therefore, is to master the technique of his craft. This can be accomplished only by first acquiring skill in the older, established, techniques. For it is the combination of these disciplines, i.e. technique added to "inventiveness," that ultimately produce a work of art, be it a painting, a poem or a symphony.

Finally, it should be emphasized that so long as our musical system remains TWELVE TONES to the octave, composers, great and small, must be bound by certain principles inherent in the chromatic scale.

Page Index

Index of Names and Titles